WHAT PEOPLE ARE SAYING ABOUT THE SERIES

An MD Examines

"We assume medical doctors' main expertise is figuring out body problems; however, Brad Burke defies assumptions that their knowledge ends there. His responses to age-old questions are simply too good to put down. His creative ideas and energy quickly engage me. Then, he walks me through a logical thought process that enables me not only to better understand the answer but to see the question better. But it's more than logic. It is a life-giving word that works its transformation beyond the healing of a broken bone or deteriorating organ. Mind, body, and soul receive healing medicine from the hands of Brad Burke. He offers good remedies for searching souls."

—DR. BRIAN C. STILLER
PRESIDENT, TYNDALE UNIVERSITY COLLEGE AND SEMINARY

"Dr. Brad Burke's series is an enormously helpful guide for all who yearn for a personal, intimate relationship with God. His critical analysis of personal spirituality is enlightening; his thoughtful answers to some of our toughest questions are both provocative and compelling; his insights into the rising twenty-first-century generation are perceptive; his medical perspective is fascinating; but most of all, his portrayal of the only true God is profound."

—DR. WILLIAM J. MCRAE
PRESIDENT EMERITUS, TYNDALE UNIVERSITY COLLEGE AND SEMINARY

"Doctor Brad's pen is sharper than his scalpel. His stories gripped me from page one. His honest search for answers to the mysteries of miracles, suffering, evil, and the existence of God is not just entertaining, it is immensely helpful and practical."

—PHIL CALLAWAY
SPEAKER, AUTHOR OF *LAUGHING MATTERS*

AN MD EXAMINES SERIES

Is God Obsolete?

Why Doesn't God Stop Evil?

Does God Still Do Miracles?

Why Does God Allow Suffering?

AN M.D. EXAMINES

WHY DOES GOD ALLOW SUFFERING?

DR. BRAD BURKE

Victor®
The Bible Teacher's Teacher

COOK COMMUNICATIONS MINISTRIES
Colorado Springs, Colorado • Paris, Ontario
KINGSWAY COMMUNICATIONS LTD
Eastbourne, England

Victor® is an imprint of
Cook Communications Ministries, Colorado Springs, CO 80918
Cook Communications, Paris, Ontario
Kingsway Communications, Eastbourne, England

WHY DOES GOD ALLOW SUFFERING?
© 2006 by Brad Burke

Published in association with the literary agency of Les Stobbe, 300
Doubleday Road, Tryon, NC 28782.

The Web addresses (URLs) recommended throughout this book are solely
offered as a resource to the reader. The citation of these Web sites does not
in any way imply an endorsement on the part of the author or the publisher,
nor does the author or publisher vouch for their content for the life of this
book.

Cover Design: Marks & Whetstone
Cover Photo: Getty Images

First Printing, 2006
Printed in the United States of America

1 2 3 4 5 6 7 8 9 10 Printing/Year 10 09 08 07 06

All Scripture quotations, unless otherwise noted, are taken from the *Holy
Bible, New International Version*®. *NIV*®. Copyright © 1973, 1978, 1984 by
International Bible Society. Used by permission of Zondervan. All rights
reserved. Scripture quotations marked NLT are from the *Holy Bible, New
Living Translation*, copyright © 1996. Used by permission of Tyndale House
Publishers, Inc., Wheaton, Illinois 60189. All rights reserved; quotations
marked NASB are taken from the *New American Standard Bible*, © Copyright
1960, 1995 by The Lockman Foundation. Used by permission; and quotations marked KJV are taken from the King James Version of the Bible. (Public
Domain.) Italics in Scripture are added by the author for emphasis.

ISBN-13: 978-0-7814-4283-1
ISBN-10: 0-7814-4283-4

LCCN: 2006923057

To my parents, David and Lucille,
who, by God's grace,
instilled within me a passion
for memorization and
meditation on Scripture

*Understanding God, for the dedicated
and faithful believer, is a day-by-day,
hour-by-hour, mind-, heart-, and
soul-grappling journey, yielding
priceless and unfathomable treasures …
sometimes by the minute … sometimes
when the saint is least expecting it.…*

CONTENTS

Acknowledgments 8

Introduction: Were You Away Then? 11

1. Suffering: God's Will or the Devil's? 17

2. The "Sovereignty of Satan" Lie 29

3. When Our Children Die 39

4. "You Have a Lot of Explaining to Do, God!" 55

5. Is God Punishing Me? 71

6. The Ultimate Reason We Suffer. 85

7. Seeing the Complete Sunset 105

8. Solomon's Clues. 125

Scenes from the Journey Ahead 141

Readers' Guide. 145

Notes. 151

ACKNOWLEDGMENTS

My second career as a writer unexpectedly began in my second year of medical school when I stumbled into the creative world of screenwriting. In a sense, An MD Examines came together remarkably like a major Hollywood film, complete with an executive producer, coproducers, editors, directors, a film studio, a screenwriter—even actors and actresses. Using the film analogy, here are the "rolling credits."

I must begin by thanking my Executive Producer on this extensive project, my Lord and heavenly Father. The astonishing way in which God brought all these talented individuals together blows the fuses in my mind. Whether or not this production wins an Oscar here on earth, God, and God alone, deserves all the glory.

Heather Gemmen, my brilliant producer and content editor, rocks! She enthusiastically presented this project to the studio, Cook Communications. My exceedingly wise coproducer, trusted friend, and mentor for more than twenty-five years, Garry Jenkins, helped steer me clear of false doctrine and "fluff."

ACKNOWLEDGMENTS

Craig Bubeck, like an experienced Tinseltown director, finely directed the thematic and visual components of this project at Cook. And the assistant director, Diane Gardner, and film publicist, Michele Tennesen, smoothly coordinated events, meetings, and communiqué between location shoots. There are so many others at Cook who played key roles; I thank them so much for their dedication to spreading God's truth around the world!

Every film needs a good editor. In addition to those mentioned above, Audrey Dorsch worked her own movie magic and brought the scenes together seamlessly.

Script consultants can make or break a film. Several provided valuable advice from scene one to "The End": Garry and Matt Jenkins, Sherri Spence, Dr. Val Jones, Wendy Elaine Nelles, and my parents. God provided other consultants for the production at key times, including world-renowned surgeon and author Dr. Paul Brand.

The Word Guild, the largest Christian writing association in Canada, played the role of a Hollywood talent agency perfectly, bringing together the screenwriter with the editors, producer, script consultant, agent, and even the production company for this powerful movie.

And what's a film without the actors and actresses? My sincere thanks also goes out to all those individuals who brought this film to life by allowing the world to see their inspiring stories.

I am grateful to Les Stobbe, my hardworking agent who helped make this series possible. My heartfelt appreciation also goes to my parents, David and Lucille, whose understanding and support during those tough years when I took a half-decade sabbatical from medicine to write this series ensured my success. I love them both very much.

In almost every film there is a love interest. To Erin, my beautiful wife, I'm looking forward to serving the Lord together for the rest of our lives.

And finally, to my brother Darryl (a stunt coordinator in training) who told me in 1999 that one day I would write a book—and I laughed ...

I apologize.

Dear God,

My family and me went to Germany last summer. We stopped at those camp places where a lot of people died. My question is—did you know about this? Were you away then?

Please answer when you can.[1]

—CINDY ELLEN (AGE 11)

WERE YOU AWAY THEN?

I stood motionlessly by her graveside, asking the inescapable question: Why?

When life hurts, helplessness often takes over the helm and routine and pleasure jump ship. The loss of a beloved child, a soul mate, a sacrificing parent, or an endeared grandparent abruptly halts the mellow voyage of life, transforming the shimmering waves of happiness into towering waves of sorrow. Nothing we do, nothing we say, nothing we possess can bring our loved ones back. Memories both comfort and pain us. Questions both flee and haunt us. Answers both calm and anger us.

Often it isn't long before we find ourselves overboard, fighting to stay afloat amid the dark and foreboding waters of despair. Sometimes the waters are familiar to us, but no friendlier. We've survived them before. We've gone down time and again ... and somehow found the strength to resurface—gasping for answers. But each time is a little different. Every crashing wave of grief pounds us into the ocean floor a little differently, contorting, spinning, and tumbling us head over heels, stopping just long enough to allow us to resurface so it can pound us again.

WHY DOES GOD ALLOW SUFFERING?

Perhaps you've never experienced the heartrending loss of someone close to you. But make no mistake, in life's game of hide-and-seek, suffering will eventually find you; it's only a matter of time. The only place one can safely hide is in the grave, and for those who have rejected God, even this is an illusion. Your unutterable suffering may be a devastating divorce, a child with cerebral palsy, an unrelenting ache deep in your back, abandonment by your mother or father, the ruinous loss of your cherished possessions in a fire, or the painful memories of abuse suffered as a child. Professor and author Dr. Edward Kuhlman (no connection to the faith healer, Kathryn Kuhlman), who lost his sixteen-year-old son to cancer, bared his soul in his book *An Overwhelming Interference*. "No one escapes life without experiencing pain," wrote Kuhlman, "although many become preoccupied with attempts to alleviate it. Pain is the overriding, inexplicable condition of life."[2]

Indeed, pain and adversity hold no prejudices. A good friend of mine, in his capacity with the Canadian government, had the rare opportunity to meet Princess Diana on one of her last visits to Canada. Shielded from the press, he met with the Princess and described her as personable, shy, soft-spoken, down-to-earth—yet restless. She asked my friend and his fiancée about their upcoming wedding plans, making the comment about how expensive weddings are these days (a bit funny considering the cost of her own wedding). And she laughingly joked about sneaking away from the press outside to get a few beers with him and his officers. My friend said she came across as a "very normal person," and he remarked, "In hindsight, I wonder if at some level, in her genuine desire to discuss our 'boring plain lives,' she wasn't longing for that."

Maybe the Princess really was just like the average person in many ways. The world's favorite Princess battled bulimia, wrestled with feelings of insecurity, experienced family feuds, and lived through a broken marriage. And at the age of thirty-seven her seemingly "fairy-tale life" reached the final line in the final chapter in a tragic Paris car crash. Even the most popular of England's royal family—the most popular and well-loved person in the world at that time—could not escape the vice-grip of pain, suffering, and death.

INTRODUCTION

As I stood by my grandmother's graveside, staring blankly at her suspended coffin, the question was grinding through my head: *Why?* Toward the end of her life, my grandmother's final dream was to hold in her arms her first great-grandchild. When my sister became pregnant for the first time, you can imagine just how excited my grandmother became. She knew that her dream would be realized in a matter of months. But less than two weeks before my sister gave birth to her first baby boy, Joshua, my grandmother, at the age of seventy-two, died of cancer.

The minister at her funeral remarked that one life was ending and in a short time another would be beginning. The words left an indelible mark on my consciousness, and I wondered to myself, *Why, God? My grandmother faithfully served and worshipped you for decades, and you couldn't give her just two more weeks to see her first great-grandchild? You allowed Simeon, the righteous and devout saint, to live until he could hold the Messiah (see Luke 2:25–35). Why, God, couldn't you have spared her life for just fourteen more days? It would have meant so much to her. We weren't demanding a miracle—just two weeks. How hard would that have been?*

But, as in Job's situation, God never answered our questions. My grandmother courageously battled breast cancer, undergoing a mastectomy and the painful aftermath of radiation—only to find later that she was filled with more cancer from an unknown source. The explosively dividing cancer cells finally won out. The pain and abdominal bloating grew intense. And she spent her final days on morphine in the hospital where I had trained during medical school.

She was my last living grandparent, and there was nothing she wouldn't do for me. But in the end, I couldn't even be there for her. I was isolated three thousand miles away in Los Angeles, working day and night in my surgery residency. One summer evening, my uncle called to tell me she had passed away. The director of the Cedar's Sinai Medical Center surgery program kindly allowed me some time off, and I flew back to Canada for her funeral.

When one life is suddenly cut short, unanswerable questions inevitably surface. When millions of innocent lives are quickly snuffed out—as in a holocaust—someone has to be blamed. I remember visiting the site of the World War II Nazi Mauthausen concentration camp in the Austrian countryside where an estimated 120,000–180,000 men, women, and children died in one of history's ugliest scenes. I walked up the 186 stone steps, known as "The Stairs of Death," where undernourished prisoners were forced to march up with huge granite blocks on their backs, some weighing more than seventy-five pounds. Sometimes the blocks would slip off their backs, crushing the bones of those struggling behind. The tortured prisoners were forced to climb up and down the steps until they died. I gazed down into the rock quarry where many prisoners were pushed to their death from the jagged cliff 100–150 feet above. Even Auschwitz captives were horrified at the thought of ending up at Mauthausen.

I stood in the basement gas chamber where the SS had herded 120 people at a time to be gassed to death. I ran my hands over the dissecting table where SS doctors performed grotesque "experiments" on live patients. I gazed into the crematorium where tens of thousands of bodies were disposed of. I stood on the roll-call square where men, women, and children were shot and clubbed to death—some mauled by dogs. Selected individuals were stripped naked, doused with icy water, and left to freeze to death in the bitter cold.

Most of those who died at the hands of the Nazis were Jews, numbering approximately six million in total. Since the holocaust, convicting fists have been shaken at God for allowing one of the most heinous crimes in history to unfold. The Jews were God's chosen people—his selected ambassadors to the world; but where was God in their suffering? Where was God in these horrible, unimaginable atrocities? Where was Jehovah when the SS officers were clubbing, gassing, shooting, and torturing millions of Jews to death—exterminating them like ants with the goal of developing a "Master Race"? No wonder little Cindy Ellen wrote to God in her letter, "Did you know about this? Were you away then?"

Most of us probably have never sat down to write an actual letter to God. But if we did, I think a good number of us would pour out our hearts to the Almighty like the patriarch Job, telling God how much we are suffering and that we've done nothing to deserve it. And like Cindy Ellen, we might ask God the very same questions: "Did you know about this? Were you away then?"

Where is God in my suffering? Perhaps no other question has

bewildered, disheartened, and angered saints more. Maybe this is the one unanswered question you've been asking all along on your journey. How can we reconcile in our minds an all-powerful, loving heavenly Father who would allow his children to suffer to such awful extremes? Why would God take the life of my loved one? And why does God seem so distant when I need him the most? These tough questions could very well have been the catalyst that led you to pick up this book series.

The questions surrounding God and our suffering represent some of the most personal, heartrending, and difficult questions ever asked in all of history. In arranging our stepping-stones it will take all the spiritual wisdom, understanding, and determination we can muster to advance on our journey. Again, I don't have all the answers, but someone infinitely wiser and more knowledgeable than me does—and many of these answers are provided for us throughout the pages of Scripture.

God often shares with us in an intimate manner what he is thinking. The problem is, we sometimes behave like little children, holding our hands over our ears, pretending we can't hear him. More often, though, we act like grown adults. The answers in God's Word are so contrary to our humanistic reasoning, we automatically assume they can't be right. But these are all reasons why God lovingly gave us the Bible. If we could intuitively figure out all the answers to the really tough questions on suffering, why would we need his supernatural revelation?

I must forewarn you that the upcoming material may be a little disturbing. You may even find yourself becoming rather irritated or even downright angry with me. I totally understand. Rather like the patriarch Jacob, I wrestled with these truths for several nights before God finally humbled me to the point where I could see life more through his eyes and less through mine. God's truth surrounding suffering is certainly not easy to comprehend. The message of this book will be very difficult to accept … but ultimately freeing. For the truth will set you free from the guilt, discouragement, anxiety, bitterness, anger, and confusion you may be experiencing in your suffering.

We may not get all the way across this particular raging river in this book; but I think if we can get far enough across to see the other side more clearly, I believe it will have all been worthwhile.

The fact of suffering undoubtedly constitutes the single greatest challenge to the Christian faith.[1]

—JOHN STOTT

1
SUFFERING: GOD'S WILL OR THE DEVIL'S?

As I write this, my friend Andrew[†], a young Christian man involved in our men's Bible study group, is experiencing devastating hardships. Married for less than a year, his wife, whom he loved deeply, suddenly walked out of the marriage, leaving him with a broken heart and thousands of dollars of debt. Nothing would change her mind. Nothing Andrew could do made any difference. Struggling to make ends meet while paying off hefty bills to lawyers, credit-card and car companies, he was forced to sell some of his possessions. He struggled to overcome demoralizing feelings of anger, bitterness, and loneliness. He shared with me one day, "The hurt is indescribable."

At the same time, his pastor was preaching on the topic of prosperity and happiness. "God wants you to be wealthy!" his pastor proclaimed. "It is not God's will or his plan for your life that you suffer in any way. God wants you to only have the best! Suffering is not part of God's agenda—but the Devil's."

---

† The name has been changed.

WHY DOES GOD ALLOW SUFFERING?

According to this happiness theology (or party-life theology, as I call it), Andrew must have been doing something terribly wrong. He wasn't bubbling over with happiness; he was besieged in the unforgiving trenches of misery with debt, lawyers, feelings of bitterness, and incredible hurt. Andrew knew he hadn't done anything to deserve this vicious adversity in his life. But here was his pastor, up at the pulpit almost every Sunday, preaching that God wants every Christian to be only happy, healthy, prosperous, and free of all adversity. Instead of helping to remove the double-edged dagger lodged in Andrew's heart, his pastor drove another dagger in right beside it. Did this unwitting shepherd realize the added pain he was inflicting on his flock?

Every day around the world, from radio, television, books, and the pulpit, similar messages are pulverizing devastated Christians trying to get back on their feet. Couples struggling with the stigma of infertility or multiple miscarriages are being scolded because they "lack enough faith"—otherwise God would give them children. Families living in the shackles of poverty are told they must be sinning for God not to bless them financially. Believers suffering tremendously with heart disease, diabetes, cancer, and paralysis from a stroke are being told God is judging them for sin and their itsy-bitsy faith. A church leader told one heartbroken mother that the reason her teenage son tragically died of diabetes was that God was punishing her. Consumed with guilt, she and her husband were driven to despair by a pastor who "controlled her congregation with fear."[2] Another couple, grieving the loss of their stillborn baby, was told that their sin of fear was responsible for their baby's death, and that they "did not have enough faith to believe the baby could be risen from the dead."[3]

Hurting and grieving Christians all over the world are turning to the church for answers and comfort ... but are frequently being pushed away by unbiblical advice from fellow Christians who know very little about how to handle suffering—and by a fairy-tale prosperity theology that only inflicts further pain and guilt. Andrew, the young man whose wife walked out on him, shared with me that this theology being shoved in his face almost drove him to turn his back completely on God.[4]

SUFFERING: GOD'S WILL OR THE DEVIL'S?

What a sickening tragedy this is! What a heartless, hateful, and unscriptural thing to do, preaching at those suffering deeply, "It's all your fault!" or "Just trust God and all your suffering will disappear." Instead of comforting fellow Christians who are in distress, we often castigate them. Where is the Christian love that Christ commands? Where is the kindness? Where is the goodness that our hurting brothers and sisters need? Where is the understanding of God? Where is the understanding of his Word? "But the fruit of the Spirit is love, joy, peace, patience, kindness, goodness, faithfulness, gentleness and self-control" (Gal. 5:22–23; see also 6:10).

Earlier in our journey we discovered that sickness and poverty are usually *not* the believer's personal fault. When the disciples came across a man blind from birth (and likely dirt poor), they asked, "'Who sinned, this man or his parents, that he was born blind?' 'Neither this man nor his parents sinned,' said Jesus, 'but this happened so that the work of God might be displayed in his life'" (John 9:2–3).

James says,

> Listen, my dear brothers: Has not God chosen those who are
> poor in the eyes of the world to be rich in faith and to inherit
> the kingdom he promised those who love him? (2:5)

Taking a journey through the Scriptures, we discover that suffering is par for life. The story of Job alone completely annihilates the popular party-life theology. God asked Satan, "Have you considered my servant Job? There is no one on earth like him; he is blameless and upright, a man who fears God and shuns evil" (Job 1:8). Job was such a godly man that every time his sons and daughters threw a party, he would offer a sacrifice, pleading with God to forgive his children of any sin, just in case they had cursed God in some way in their hearts (vv. 4–5). If Job was so diligent in appealing for God's forgiveness for the secret sins he wasn't even sure his kids committed, imagine just how diligent he would have been in ridding his own heart of sin.

Yet it was God's will that Job suffer tidal waves of adversity— tragedies so awful that they are unfathomable to most of us. God gave

WHY DOES GOD ALLOW SUFFERING?

Satan permission to strip away all the most precious possessions of Job, described as "the greatest man among all the people of the East" (v. 3). One day a messenger, out of breath, ran up to Job, "The Sabeans killed your servants and stole your thousand oxen and five hundred donkeys!" Before he could end his sentence, another messenger rushed up, "A fireball from heaven burned up your servants and burned your seven thousand sheep to a crisp!" While he was still speaking, another courier raced up, "Job, the Chaldeans swooped in, murdered all your servants and stole your three thousand camels!" Before the last syllable was off his tongue, a fourth messenger arrived, "A mighty wind swept down and blew in the walls of your eldest son's home. Your seven sons and three daughters—Job, I don't know how to say this … *they're all dead.* I'm the only one who escaped" (see vv. 2–3, 13–19).

Picture yourself for a moment in Job's sandals. Imagine learning within the span of a couple of minutes that you had lost almost everything you owned, and that your seven sons and three daughters, whom you loved with all your heart, whom you earnestly prayed for every day, had all tragically died. Everything you loved and had worked for in life, except your wife, was now gone. And if that were not enough, you would soon find yourself covered from head to toe with painful, scaly, and worm-contaminated sores. Very few in this world have suffered so much loss so quickly. Was it God's will that Job suffer deeply? Studying the Scriptures, we see that obviously it was.

Yet proponents of this party-life theology, particularly those in the Word–Faith charismatic movement, claim that Job was a bullheaded man with a "big mouth" who got what was coming to him. (Not even the tabloids could do a better job of trashing Job's character.) Popular televangelist Benny Hinn has since relented from his position, saying that when he gets to heaven he's going to apologize to Job for all the nasty things he has said about him.[5]

Similar trash talk has been hurled at God's greatest and most influential preacher, the apostle Paul. After his conversion, we don't read of one single sin that Paul committed. (Though I'm not saying that Paul was sinless.) Paul said he served God "with a clear conscience" (2 Tim. 1:3) that could be vouched for by the indwelling Holy Spirit (see Rom.

9:1). Yet those who try to explain why Paul suffered the "thorn in the flesh" have dubbed the apostle a proud, faithless sinner. The superapostle pleaded with God to remove this thorn, but God instead replied, "My grace is sufficient for you, for my power is made perfect in weakness" (2 Cor. 12:9). Like almost all the disciples, Paul later died a martyr's death, likely being beheaded in a Roman prison. Was it God's will that Paul suffer? Obviously it was.

What about God's own Son, Jesus Christ? Unbelievably, some Word–Faith teachers argue that God's hands were tied when it came to Christ's gruesome death. Another popular televangelist, Kenneth Copeland, says this:

> I was shocked when I found out who the biggest failure in the Bible actually is.… The biggest one in the whole Bible is God.… Now, the reason you don't think of God as a failure is He never said He's a failure. And you're not a failure till you say you're one.[6]

This is utter heresy! No wonder Copeland believes "Satan *conquered* Jesus on the Cross."[7] In Copeland's mind, God was a failure to begin with. Like so many other Word–Faith teachers, Copeland believes that it was never God's intention for Christ to die. "In fact, many Faith teachers claim that Christ's torture by all the demons of hell was a 'ransom' God paid to Satan so that He could get back into a universe from which He had been banished."[8] Is it any wonder, then, that these false teachers are the same ones preaching that all your suffering is *your fault?*

In striking contrast to Copeland's comments, we read in Scripture that it was God's plan from all eternity that his Son come to earth to suffer and die a grotesque and painful death on the cross (see 2 Tim. 1:9). God, not Satan, even raised to power the exact persons he allowed to murder Christ (see John 19:11; Acts 2:23; 4:27–28). God had planned down to the minutest detail how he would send his only Son to earth to die and suffer for our sins—long before he even created Satan. Furthermore, Jesus was not being punished for something *he* did. He took upon himself the punishment for something *we* did. Dr. Kuhlman asserts, "The startling aspect of suffering is that it is a vital part (*the* vital part!) of God's redemptive plan."[9] Was it God's will that Christ suffer such a heinous death? Clearly it was.

Regarding most faith healers' party-life theology, John MacArthur writes in his book *The Power of Suffering:*

> Such a theology of nonsuffering, if carried to its logical extreme, must claim that Jesus was out of God's will when He died on the cross. That thinking is more than bad logic, it is downright heretical.[10]

From Genesis through Revelation, godly men and women viewed suffering as part of God's will. With regard to Moses, the prince of Egypt, the writer of Hebrews says, "He regarded disgrace for the sake of Christ as of greater value than the treasures of Egypt, because he was looking ahead to his reward" (Heb. 11:26).

When Job's wife urged him to "Curse God and die!" Job replied, "You are talking like a foolish woman. Shall we accept good from God, and not trouble?" (Job 2:9–10). Isaiah records God's very words: "I form the light and create darkness, I bring prosperity and create disaster; I, the LORD, do all these things" (Isa. 45:7).

The wisdom writer of Ecclesiastes says:

> Consider what God has done: Who can straighten what he has made crooked? When times are good, be happy; but when times are bad, consider: God has made the one as well as the other. Therefore, a man cannot discover anything about his future. (7:13–14)

Christ even told his followers to expect suffering: "Blessed are those who are persecuted because of righteousness, for theirs is the kingdom of heaven. Blessed are you when people insult you, persecute you and falsely say all kinds of evil against you because of me" (Matt. 5:10–11). "In this world you will have trouble. But take heart! I have overcome the world" (John 16:33b). "Remember the words I spoke to you," said Christ. "'No servant is greater than his master.' If they persecuted me, they will persecute you also" (John 15:20a).

SUFFERING: GOD'S WILL OR THE DEVIL'S?

The believers in Tyre pleaded with the apostle Paul not to journey to Jerusalem, a city fraught with lurking dangers. Paul, flustered that his flock could not understand that this was the will of God (see Acts 20:22; 21:14; 23:11), replied, "Why all this weeping? You are breaking my heart! For I am ready not only to be jailed at Jerusalem but also to die for the sake of the Lord Jesus" (Acts 21:13 NLT). At the very beginning, Christ said to Ananias, "I will show [Paul] how much he must suffer for my name" (Acts 9:16). And suffer he did!

Paul, who unbelievably survived thirty-nine lashes on five occasions, three shipwrecks, a stoning (being left for dead), several imprisonments, prejudice, hunger, thirst, and cold, didn't question his faith because he was facing adversity in life; instead, he used it as proof that he was doing God's will:

> Rather, as servants of God we commend ourselves in every way: in great endurance; in troubles, hardships and distresses; in beatings, imprisonments and riots; in hard work, sleepless nights and hunger; in purity, understanding, patience and kindness; in the Holy Spirit and in sincere love; … dying, and yet we live on; beaten, and yet not killed; sorrowful, yet always rejoicing; poor, yet making many rich; having nothing, and yet possessing everything. (2 Cor. 6:4–6, 9–10)

All suffering, no matter what it is, falls under the umbrella of God's permissive will. Satan may occasionally be used as a "hit man" or an instrument of such suffering, but in the end it is God who allows the tragedy as an integral part of his sovereign will.

The apostle Peter stressed this truth:

> Dear friends, do not be surprised at the painful trial you are suffering, as though something strange were happening to you. But rejoice that you participate in the sufferings of Christ, so that you may be overjoyed when his glory is revealed. If you are insulted because of the name of Christ, you are blessed, for the Spirit of glory and of God rests on you. (1 Peter 4:12–14)

WHY DOES GOD ALLOW SUFFERING?

The writer of Hebrews praised the past heroes of faith for enduring great adversity—he didn't belittle them for their suffering:

> Some faced jeers and flogging, while still others were chained and put in prison. They were stoned; they were sawed in two; they were put to death by the sword. They went about in sheepskins and goatskins, destitute, persecuted and mistreated—the world was not worthy of them. They wandered in deserts and mountains, and in caves and holes in the ground. These were all commended for their faith, yet none of them received what had been promised. God had planned something better for us so that only together with us would they be made perfect. (Heb. 11:36–40)

Paul goes so far as to say that believers are "destined" for tribulations, trials, and afflictions (see 1 Thess. 3:3). The Scriptures are replete with verses speaking of adversity in a positive light, as part of God's will—expected troubles that we will face as we live for Christ in a fallen and sin-cursed world.††

Remember Jim Bakker, the former televangelist and founder of the PTL (Praise the Lord) empire who had a yearly income of thirty million dollars, a forty-room mansion, twelve cars, and an air-conditioned doghouse? Bakker for years taught this fairy-tale, health-and-prosperity theology, teaching that suffering is not part of God's agenda, that it is God's will for every believer to be perfectly healthy, enormously rich, and trouble free. But after studying the Bible (while spending five years in prison on fraud charges), Bakker reached a much different conclusion: "This used to be my motto: Make it happen. I was wrong," he said.[11] In a commencement address, Bakker pleaded from the heart to the graduates, "Don't follow the world. Don't give in to materialism…. If you want to be a man of God, you're going to go through hell."[12] Bakker was

---

†† See Gen. 3:16–19; 45:5–8; 50:20; Ps. 119:71; Matt. 5:10; 16:24–25; John 15:18–21; 16:2; Acts 7; 9:16; Rom. 5:3–5; 8:17–18; 1 Thess. 1:6–7; 2 Thess. 1:4; Gal. 6:2; 2 Cor. 1:5; 4:16–18; 12:10; Phil. 1:29–30; 3:10; 1 Peter 1:6–7; 2:20–23; 4:1–2; 5:8–10; 2 Tim. 2:3; 3:10–12; James 1:2–4; 5:10–11; Rev. 2:9–10.

echoing the apostle Paul's words to Timothy: "In fact, everyone who wants to live a godly life in Christ Jesus will be persecuted" (2 Tim. 3:12).

"More Christians have died for their faith in the 20th century than in the previous nineteen centuries combined."[13] More Christians than ever around the world are suffering persecution and adversity at this very moment.[14] Muslims and hard-line communists outside the West are torturing, maiming, imprisoning, raping, burning, selling into slavery, and executing scores of Christians every single hour.

Paul Marshall, author of *Their Blood Cries Out,* estimates that "three-fourths of all Christians live outside the West. It may be the largest Third World religion."[15] According to what many faith healers preach then, I guess their nonsuffering theology doesn't extend to most of our loyal brothers and sisters suffering the unspeakable atrocities of religious persecution on the other side of the world. I must have missed the Scripture verse that says only Christians *in the West* have the authority to "speak the word" and instantly drive away sickness, poverty, and evil.

Not only are such false teachers seemingly ignorant of the affairs of Christians on the other side of the globe, they are apparently ignorant of their brothers and sisters living in their own backyards. Stop and take an honest look around you. Millions of people, including numerous godly Christians, in North America and Europe are in poor health, living below the poverty line, or suffering some type of horrible adversity. If God promises every single believer only health, wealth, and happiness, my question is, *Where is it?* When is this divine agenda of untold riches and perfect health finally going to kick in around the globe? When is God going to get serious with his alleged promise that Christians will never suffer?

Jim Bakker hits the nail on the head when he admits:

> I had gotten my sermons from other people. The Bible warns about the shepherds who get their messages from each other. I think today the reason we have another gospel and another Jesus being preached is because men have gotten their sermons from each other and from motivational teaching. A lot of what's being taught today is simply motivational teaching with a few Scriptures put to it.[16]

WHY DOES GOD ALLOW SUFFERING?

Why is this erroneous "health and wealth" doctrine flourishing like an out-of-control weed in the church today? Because leaders, restless for the world's "stuff" of fame, fortune, and TV ratings, have abandoned the Bible and started fertilizing the thoughts in their sermons, books, radio, and TV messages with the same old worthless manure from yesterday's televangelists. In some movements we have the blind (famous faith healers) leading the faith-healer wannabes (church pastors) leading the disillusioned (the people hearing the pastors' messages).

As a result, "We've trivialized God," says Christian psychologist and author Larry Crabb. Regarding a roster of current best sellers, Crabb remarked, "Most of these books assume God is the butler who serves you for one reason: to give you a happy life. We've turned him into a divine Prozac."[17]

Dear friends, if your pastor is trivializing God by rehashing from televangelists the same old health-and-wealth gospel and wrapping it all together in a motivational teaching shell, I encourage you to gently challenge your pastor with the verses presented earlier. Maybe you could even meet with the board of elders. If nothing works, I suggest finding a church that preaches God's Word. (This is the route my friend Andrew finally took.) If your pastor is continually teaching that God, like some sort of "divine Prozac," wants your Christian life to be only a bed of roses, leave your church and find a pastor who gets his material from the one true source—the inerrant and authoritative Word of God.

IF GOD PROMISES EVERY SINGLE BELIEVER ONLY HEALTH, WEALTH, AND HAPPINESS, MY QUESTION IS, *WHERE IS IT?* WHEN IS GOD GOING TO GET SERIOUS WITH HIS ALLEGED PROMISE THAT CHRISTIANS WILL NEVER SUFFER?

Therefore, those also who suffer according to the will of God shall entrust their souls to a faithful Creator in doing what is right.

—1 PETER 4:19 NASB

2
THE "SOVEREIGNTY OF SATAN" LIE

The world misunderstands Satan almost as much it misunderstands God. Some believers live in constant fear of being attacked by the evil destroyer. They worry that Satan is trying to bankrupt them; they fear that Satan might come in and suffocate their infant as the baby sleeps; they dread the day when the Devil might strike them with cancer; they worry that Satan will lure away their spouse or send their car hurtling over a precipice. Consequently, these individuals habitually "plead the blood of Christ" in every room of their home; they sprinkle or wipe special oils on their door frames to keep the Devil out; and they go to Herculean extremes to try to "bind Satan."

It's really not surprising that most of the confusion about Satan has arisen in the lives of those who possess a shallow understanding of God's sovereignty. If you've been sheltered from particular branches of the charismatic movement, you might be quite shocked and appalled at what's actually being taught by some men and women.[1]

The false doctrine goes something like this: When God cast Satan down to earth, the Devil caused Adam to sin, and in the process, Satan took control of the entire world. The Devil, in a sense, held the earth hostage from God. As some authors have pointed out, Satan has become the criminal and God the victim. For God to get back what he had created, he needed to make a pact with Abram. As stated by Benny Hinn, God allegedly told Abram that he, the Almighty Creator of the universe, "could not touch this earth till a man gave it back to Him."[2]

Many, like Hinn, who are caught up in the dangerous web of the charismatic Word–Faith faction, have borrowed their heretical doctrine from the father of the whole movement, E. W. Kenyon. It was Kenyon who made famous the teaching that when God made his covenant with Abram, Abram got wealth, health, and prosperity, and God, in exchange, got permission and the means necessary to gain entrance back to earth.[3] Supposedly, God still needs us to "speak the Word" before he can act according to his stipulated laws.

The late popular charismatic teacher Kenneth E. Hagin Sr., who once said, "You are as much the incarnation of God as Jesus Christ was,"[4] recounts an alleged chat he had with God one day. Frequently interrupting the pair, however, was Satan. Hagin, having had enough, finally asked God to shut the Devil up. But God told Hagin he couldn't. So Hagin commanded the Devil to keep silent! According to Hagin, "Jesus looked at me, and said, 'If you hadn't done anything about that, I couldn't have.'"[5]

Another popular TV evangelist, Kenneth Copeland, states this:

> The Bible says that God gave this earth to the sons of men … and when [Adam] turned and gave that dominion to Satan, look where it left God. It left Him on the outside looking in.… He had no legal right to do anything about it, did He? … He had injected Himself illegally into the earth—what Satan had intended for Him to do was to fall for it—pull off an illegal act and turn the light off on God, and subordinate God to himself.… He intended to get God into such a trap that He couldn't get out.[6]

Such nonsense and blasphemy is widely accepted as truth in some charismatic circles. It fits into the pervasive, heretical doctrine labeled by some as "the sovereignty of Satan"—the idea that Satan, not God, is really in control of the events around us, that Satan is constantly messing up God's plan, causing all manner of suffering; and God, apparently with his hands tied and his feet in cement, needs our prayers—our permission—to accomplish anything good. This erroneous doctrine runs contrary to the entire Bible, including Psalm 24:1 "The earth is the LORD's, and everything in it, the world, and all who live in it."

Bits and pieces of this unbiblical doctrine have subtly infiltrated and influenced the works of many authors. And a good many of their books have made their way into nearly every evangelical denomination.

For example, Wesley L. Duewel, in his book *Touch the World Through Prayer,* writes, "God's eternal plan was interrupted by Satan. This interruption has lasted for several thousand years."[7] Duewel also maintains that we have the authority to bind Satan.[8]

Dutch Sheets, in his book *Intercessory Prayer,* writes, "Without question, *humans were forever to be God's link to authority and activity on the earth.*"[9] "The reality of it," says Sheets, "is that sometimes [God] cannot do what we've asked because we have not given Him enough power in our prayer times to get it done."[10] Like Duewel, Sheets maintains that we have authority to tread on, bind, and defeat Satan.[11] Although I disagree with *this* teaching, both Duewel and Sheets have many good things to say about prayer in their books.

Those who buy fully into this erroneous "Sovereignty of Satan" doctrine often live life in constant fear. These souls can't fully trust God to protect them from demonic attacks because God isn't in complete control. Our Creator needs our help to do anything, they claim, since Satan is out of control and running the show.

Tell me this: Have you ever seen a vicious, bloodthirsty pit bull or Doberman tied to a heavy chain? No matter how hard the powerful beast pushes, pulls, strains, snarls, and froths against the solid metal, it can't go one inch beyond its bounds. The Scriptures teach us over and over again that God, and God alone, is the absolute sovereign ruler of the entire universe. God says, "*My* purpose will stand, and *I* will do all that *I* please" (Isa. 46:10b). God holds the end of a heavy chain that is tied tight around Satan's neck, and Satan cannot tread one inch outside ιe bounds that God allows. God can jerk the Devil here and there, wherever, however, and whenever he wants. Satan can only act upon strict permission from his master.

If you have any doubts, just read the story of Job. Not only did the Devil have to answer to God for his whereabouts, but the Devil had to

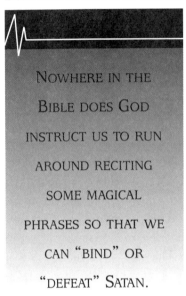

NOWHERE IN THE BIBLE DOES GOD INSTRUCT US TO RUN AROUND RECITING SOME MAGICAL PHRASES SO THAT WE CAN "BIND" OR "DEFEAT" SATAN.

get specific permission from God on two separate occasions before he could touch Job, his family, and his possessions (see Job 1:6–12; 2:4–7). In Satan's temptation of Jesus, he even acknowledges that any power and splendor he has was given to him (obviously, by God; see Luke 4:6). Satan cannot touch you in any way whatsoever unless God first gives him permission (see also Luke 22:31).

Now, it is true that God sometimes allows Satan to afflict us with illness (see Job 2:6–7), cause adversity in our lives (see 2 Cor. 12:7), tempt us (see 1 Thess. 3:5), and seemingly hinder us from spreading the gospel (see 1 Thess. 2:18). And God allows all these trials and suffering for a special purpose in his sovereign plan (see Rom. 8:28; 1 Cor. 5:5).

Some may ask: "Is Satan, as in the case of Job, behind all my illnesses and adversities? Does he inflict me with migraines or pains in my back whenever I try to do something good for God?"

I suppose Satan himself could inflict you with migraines, back pain, or the like; but given that there are approximately seven billion people on earth, the chances are that he was somewhere else in the world when the pain struck. Unlike God, Satan cannot be everywhere at once. The Devil also is not all-knowing and all-powerful like our Creator. (That's not to say that his demons couldn't be close by.)

Almost all such illnesses, however, are *not* the work of Satan or his demons. How do I know? Because so many illnesses are caused from our defective genes, the environment, and psychosomatic disease. Genetics play a huge role in numerous diseases. Defects in single genes are known to be responsible for more than three thousand diseases.[12] Several disorders can be linked to more than one gene, including such common diseases as cancer, type 2 diabetes, asthma, and heart disease.[13] When the flu goes around, it strikes indiscriminately those who come into contact with someone infected. Consider also that kids suddenly grow sick on the day of a test. Workers have flare-ups of back pain when their boss asks when they'll be returning to work. Teenagers develop sore throats, headaches, and "pain in my kidneys" when asked to clean up the yard or go to visit unliked relatives.

Sometimes individuals are faking these symptoms, but usually their illnesses and pain are caused by proven mind-body mechanisms that we've adapted to prevent us from doing something that, consciously or subconsciously, we don't want to do. If someone is depressed, fearful, or guilt ridden, he or she has a much higher chance of developing pain somewhere in the body. Therefore, if believers face significantly more sickness or accidents than nonbelievers, it might be because they are setting themselves up by expecting Satan to suddenly strike when things start going well.

The chances that Satan himself is personally tempting you, causing sickness, etc., are highly unlikely. Satan gets way too much credit for stuff he doesn't do. Satan is not behind all your computer crashes, illnesses, flat tires, windstorms, marriage problems, sick pets, traffic jams, and personal acts of sin.

Those who believe that Satan is running the show often believe that God is too weak to prevent the Devil from striking someone down with illness. A young friend of mine was recently diagnosed with multiple sclerosis. She hated needles, and one of the hardest things she had to do in the beginning was give herself the necessary injections into her thigh muscle. A woman one day said to her, "This multiple sclerosis is not God's will for your life. This is the work of the enemy." To which my friend wisely replied, "If the enemy can thwart the plans that God has for my life, and overturn God's will for me, then why would I want to serve a God like that?"

WHY DOES GOD ALLOW SUFFERING?

A question that frequently arises is this: "Does God expect us to tread upon and bind Satan in an effort to end all suffering?" Did Christ confer this authority to us when he died on the cross? Those who tout the infectious and bogus "deliverance model" of spiritual warfare ideology would answer yes.

Nowhere in the Bible, though, does God instruct us to run around reciting some magical phrases so that we can "bind" or "defeat" Satan. Nowhere are we instructed to "plead the blood of Christ" in our homes and businesses to drive out demons. When God's mightiest archangel Michael was fighting with the Devil over Moses' body, did he say, "I bind you Satan"? No. Michael didn't dare utter a word against Satan. Rather, he said, "The Lord rebuke you!" (Jude v. 9). Now if God's mightiest archangel didn't have the authority and power at that instant to "bind" Satan, what makes some believers think they do?

When the messenger of Satan was sent to torment the apostle Paul, did Paul lash out, "I rebuke and bind you Satan!" No. Paul pleaded with God three times to remove the "thorn" in the flesh (see 2 Cor. 12:7). But God chose not to do so. Instead, God said, "My grace is sufficient for you, for my power is made perfect in weakness" (v. 9). The disciples early on were given the authority and power by God to cast out demons, but this was only for a short length of time. Obviously, this power had left Paul by the time he received this "thorn" from Satan.

When God finally confronted Job in the end, did God shout out, "Job, you loser! All you had to do was say, 'I bind you Satan!' and all this mess would have never happened!" No. For seventy-one straight verses, God thunders out to Job from a fierce whirlwind, hammering home the truth that he, and he alone, is the all-powerful King, the all-knowing Creator, and the all-together sovereign Lord of the universe who is in *complete* control of absolutely everything at all times!

The one verse that's frequently used by proponents to argue for this unbiblical "binding" is Jesus' words: "Whatever you bind on earth will be bound in heaven, and whatever you loose on earth will be loosed in heaven" (Matt. 18:18; 16:19). This verse, however, has absolutely nothing to do with the binding or loosing of Satan. Why would someone want to loose a demon on earth—or in heaven? Studying the passage in its context, it becomes clear that the binding and loosing spoken of here refer to the church's authority in disciplinary measures carried out in accord with decisions previously made in heaven.[14] This interpretation is held by such esteemed men as W. E. Vine, Warren W. Wiersbe, Matthew Henry, John MacArthur, David Brown, Paul S. Karleen, R. C. Sproul, J. I. Packer, and John Calvin, to name a few.[15, 16]

Instead of directing us to "bind" Satan, what does God instruct us to do? "Submit yourselves, then, to God. Resist the devil, and he will flee from you" (James 4:7). Likewise, we read, "Resist [the Devil], standing firm in the faith" (1 Peter 5:9). Paul urges, "Do not give the devil an opportunity" (Eph. 4:27 NASB). Instead of trying to tie up Satan, Paul instructs believers to "Put on the full armor of God so that you can take your stand against the devil's schemes" (Eph. 6:11). God instructs us to resist the Devil with the "full armor of God"—not try to tackle the Devil with our bare hands.

Sadly, millions of believers are showing up on the spiritual battlefield naked and unprotected. Instead of submitting to God's moral will and wisdom, these believers are largely neglecting God's Word (the sword). Consequently, they are tossed to and fro by every wind of doctrine. Instead of putting on God's full armor, these souls are running around stark naked, trying to bind and defeat Satan. And do you know what Satan is doing? He's standing there on the battlefield laughing at these "nude" believers racing out at him, shouting, "I rebuke you Satan! I bind you Satan!"

Those who primarily ignore God's Word in order to chase after spectacular experiences are usually the ones most defenseless against the Devil. That's not to say that everyone who goes about trying to bind

> THE DEVIL CANNOT FORCE A TRUE BELIEVER TO SIN IN ANY WAY. IF WE AS BELIEVERS SIN, THAT SIN ORIGINATED FROM OUR LUSTS AND OUR PRIDE.

Satan neglects God's Word. But it is these vulnerable souls who are often obsessed with trying to handcuff the Devil. I honestly believe that God allows the Devil to pick off some of these individuals with "flaming arrows" (Eph. 6:16) to show the rest of us that this is *not* how we are to go about fighting spiritual battles. While Satan cannot physically possess a true believer (see Eph. 1:13), the father of lies can greatly influence defenseless Christians who refuse to take up the "shield of faith" and the "sword of the Spirit" (the Word of God).

In addition, those who believe they can bind Satan frequently use him as an excuse for their sin: "The Devil made me do it." The Devil, however, cannot force a true believer to sin in any way (see 1 Cor. 10:13). If we as believers sin, that sin originated from our lusts and our pride (see Mark 7:20–23). When Satan tempted David to sin by numbering his people (see 1 Chron. 21:1), seventy thousand Israelite men were killed in a single day as judgment from God. But did David blame Satan? David, a man after God's own heart, took full responsibility: "Then David said to God, 'I have sinned greatly by doing this. Now, I beg you, take away the guilt of your servant. I have done a very foolish thing'" (v. 8). If you sin, do what David did: Take full responsibility and don't try to blame it on the Devil. God knows better.

While Satan is referred to in the Bible as the "prince of the power of the air" (Eph. 2:2 NASB), we can take comfort and refuge in the truth that the God we serve is "the blessed and only Ruler, the King of kings and Lord of lords" (1 Tim. 6:15). The Devil may be the "prince" but our God is the "King of kings." A prince is always subservient to the king; and all power and authority that a prince holds is derived from the sovereign king and can be withdrawn at any moment. Every time the Devil acts, he is bringing more glory to God in the big picture of life. The Devil, consequently, is probably the most frustrated being on the face of the planet.

Christ's death on the cross was a preliminary victory over Satan (see Col. 2:15). Because of Christ's death, believers are no longer in bondage to sin and cannot be blinded and possessed by the Devil's power. A day is coming when Satan will be "thrown into the lake of burning sulfur" where he "will be tormented day and night for ever and ever" (Rev. 20:10). As some authors have noted, Calvary was Satan's defeat and the lake of fire is the final execution of the sentence (see Gen. 3:15; Rom. 16:20).

The moral of the story is this: Live life in obedience to God and let the master deal with his "servant" Satan. Obedience to God's Word is the key to defending yourself against the master of illusion—the "angel of light." "If you live a holy life," says John MacArthur, "Satan is already bound because, 'Greater is he that is in you than he that is in the world'"[17] (1 John 4:4 KJV). Therefore, submit yourself to God; resist the Devil; and stop trying to grab the leash out of God's hands. You're not strong enough to hold it. The Devil has not interrupted God's plan for thousands of years, and we shouldn't run around trying to bind Satan in an attempt to fix what isn't broken. God doesn't need our help in handling Satan. The Mighty One has everything under control.

Our self-existent and all-powerful heavenly Father is sovereign—not Satan. As hard as it is to understand, Satan didn't interrupt God's plan; *Satan and suffering were part of God's sovereign plan all along.*

WHY DOES GOD ALLOW SUFFERING?

*Sometimes a thunderbolt will shoot
from a clear sky; and sometimes, into the
midst of a peaceful family—without
warning of gathered storm above or slightest
tremble of earthquake beneath—will fall
a terrible fact, and from that moment
everything is changed. The air is thick with
cloud, and cannot weep itself clear. There
may come a gorgeous sunset, though.*[1]

—GEORGE MACDONALD

3
WHEN OUR CHILDREN DIE

Ron and Arlene are a beautiful, loving, and dedicated Christian couple in their late forties, living in Pickering, Ontario, Canada (just outside of Toronto). I remember many summers when Ron and Arlene would drive up to Ron's parents' tranquil lakeside cottage just a few doors down from our home. My brother, Darryl, and I would play with their two oldest boys, Vaughn and Jayson, who were close to our ages and just as reckless for adventure. Together, we darted through the trails on our dirt bikes, puttered around in paddleboats, caught frogs, and built rickety tree houses.

Since those carefree days of summer in the '70s and '80s, life has dramatically changed for Ron, Arlene, and their family. In fact, almost everything has changed.

One of the most difficult questions they now face is, "How many children do you have?"

"We have six sons," is the answer they've come to agree on. If the follow-up question is asked, "Where are they all?" or "What are they all doing?" they pause briefly in their minds, knowing that their next response will invite further painful questions and memories. "We have six sons," they answer. "Three are in heaven. And three are here with us."

Like Ron and Arlene, maybe you have lost a much-loved child or someone else just as close to you. Or perhaps you are suffering some other adversity in your life, asking the rising question through your tears: "Why, God? Why did you allow this to happen?"

If these are the questions you are struggling with, I hope and pray that you will be both encouraged and strengthened in your faith as you hear Ron and Arlene's moving story. Their heartrending loss of three sons took them through the pounding storms of heartache, guilt, pain, and physical and mental illness. But through it all, as the quotation that opened this chapter promises, God delivered a sunset of hope and transformed faith that pierced through even their darkest clouds.[2]

"I SWORE TO MY GRAVE THAT NOBODY WOULD KNOW"

"Vaughn is dead."

The first thought that came into Arlene's mind was, *Ron, this is nothing to joke about! How dare you even kid around like that about our teenage son?*

Approximately nineteen years earlier, Arlene and Ron had decided to get married when she became unexpectedly pregnant with their first child, Vaughn. They were both Christians in their late teens. An abortion wasn't an option. Besides, after living through the initial shock of the pregnancy test results, they very much wanted and loved Vaughn.

The years that followed were particularly stressful for the young couple. Moving out of their parents' homes, they purchased their own home in the Toronto area. Ron was busy with the training and exams that went along with his apprenticeship as an electrician. At the age of twenty-two he was sent out of town to work as a foreman.

In the midst of this pressure, their second son, Jayson, was born. Jayson would be the first of three sons with major childhood illnesses. He spent his first two months in the hospital, convulsing on and off. At eight months he contracted the deadly disease of meningitis, and the doctors weren't sure he would survive. But he did.

Their third son, Brent, suffered from severe asthma. As a child, he would wake up not able to breathe and was sometimes forced to stay in the hospital inside an oxygen tent for a week at a time. Through it all, Ron continued to work long hours to support his wife and sons— sometimes logging eighteen to twenty hours a day.

Over the years, Curtis, Tyler, and Greg were born. With six sons now, life, as expected, was hectic; but Vaughn, now nearing the end of his teenage years, didn't get left out. Ron and Arlene enjoyed a close relationship with their eldest son, who loved to come into their room at any hour of the night, sit on the end of their bed, and just chat about anything.

Ron's long, crazy hours of work, however, were beginning to exact a heavy toll on the marriage. They had purchased some rental buildings, and evenings were taken up repairing and fixing them. They had also started a business repairing eighteen-wheelers—only to go bankrupt after three years. Landlord-tenant hassles also consumed their time and further pushed them apart from God—and each other.

With their marriage on the brink of collapse, Arlene, who had been raised in "half a Christian home," as she put it, broke down and shared something she had sworn nobody would ever know. After eighteen years of marriage, Arlene finally disclosed to her husband one of her darkest and longest kept secrets: she had endured years of sexual abuse as a child.

Up to this point, Ron couldn't figure out why Arlene acted so strangely at times. He couldn't understand some of her personality traits, and why she refused to sleep on the side of the bed closest to the door. Now everything made sense. And it was to be a major turning point in their marriage.

The rebuilding began. But the next storm came quickly—and totally unexpectedly.

Vaughn met an attractive non-Christian girl and was determined. "I'm going to win her for the Lord." It wasn't long, however, until he was dragged down in his faith, like so many Christian teenagers who go the "missionary dating" route. He eventually withdrew from attending the early weekly communion services, becoming cold toward the things of God.

The relationship between the teenage pair eventually turned sour. Stressed out over everything, Vaughn made a half-hearted suicide attempt by swallowing a number of Tylenol pills. He then drove over to his aunt's place and threw up. (Ron and Arlene didn't learn about this until much later.) To make matters worse, this girl, now his ex-girlfriend, was harassing Vaughn, showing up unexpectedly at his school and church.

On the day of his death, Vaughn stayed home from school, complaining of the flu. Ron called at 11:00 a.m. to see how his son was feeling. There was no indication that Vaughn was stressed out. Everything seemed okay with the eighteen-year-old.

At noon Vaughn called the number of a girl he knew well, his voice sounding urgent. Her dad answered the phone, took down the number, and promised that his daughter would call back. Neighbors later reported that between 12:00 and 12:30 p.m., Vaughn had gone outside to change the oil in his car. At 3:30 p.m. Jayson came home from school—to find his older brother hanging in the basement.

The coroner put Vaughn's time of death at 12:30 p.m.

Vaughn was buried on his brother Jayson's sixteenth birthday. For several years thereafter, Jayson asked that his family not celebrate the actual day of his birthday. Even now, they choose to celebrate it on a different day.

"I CAN HANDLE THIS, MOM AND DAD"

None of Vaughn's friends or teachers could believe what had happened. Vaughn had displayed essentially no signs of depression. He always came to school with a smile on his face. He was an athletic and good-looking kid. He was very polite. In his school they tried to incorporate the disabled and mentally handicapped children into the regular classes, and Vaughn was always the first to put up his hand to volunteer to help them. His suicide came as a complete shock to everyone.

Ron and Arlene were overcome with grief. Sleepless nights, tear-drenched pillows, and questions of why wrought havoc on their emotions and their bodies. Just when the fire was being rekindled in their marriage, they lost their oldest child. Consequently, both suffered severe feelings of guilt and shame. The first thought that came into Arlene's mind was, "God took Vaughn to punish us because our son was conceived out of wedlock."

Minor disagreements, conflict, and missed bonding opportunities with their son that had once seemed trivial now haunted their minds. Arlene said, "I would second-guess everything. Was I wrong to say, 'I can't talk tonight. Let's talk tomorrow,' when he knocked on my door at 11:30 at night and I was totally exhausted? Now I wish I could somehow bring back that knock."

No one seemed prepared for what happened—including the leaders in their church. The members in their assembly were very supportive—practically, financially, and emotionally—but they had never experienced a suicide in their congregation. Ron, Arlene, their family, and their church struggled to cope with the loss.

In retrospect, the couple feels that a good deal of their suffering was self-inflicted—particularly with respect to their financial and spiritual decisions. Up until that point, they had been heavily involved in the church, attending most services, teaching Sunday school, coordinating children's meetings, leading the youth, taking them on weekend retreats, and organizing church picnics. Ron even did a bit of preaching. "We were busy," Arlene admitted, "but we weren't getting into the Word ourselves as much as we needed." Ron agreed. "Even though we were busy in the Christian realm, somehow we weren't latching onto the truth. Our focus had shifted from spiritual to material." Stressing the importance of studying God's Word, Ron felt certain that things would have turned out differently had he been a better spiritual leader in the home.

WHY DOES GOD ALLOW SUFFERING?

"After Vaughn's death we really made a genuine attempt to live a proper Christian life," said Ron. They increased the time spent studying God's Word and teaching their children God's truths. Many parents having come through a similar tragedy might have said, "Okay, God. You've got our attention. And we've changed because of it. The hurt will always be there but things can only get better from here."

Even bigger storm clouds were brewing, however, for the close-knit family.

Greg, the youngest at fifteen months old, became seriously ill. The pediatrician said he was only responding to the negative environment stressors in the home from the recent death. After months of diarrhea and painful abdominal bloating, Greg was finally diagnosed with celiac disease—a lifelong intestinal malabsorption disorder caused by intolerance to gluten, a protein found in wheat, rye, oats, and barley. His diet was severely restricted.

In addition, Vaughn's death was particularly tough on Jayson, who consequently reacted out of character on several occasions as a teenager—his rebellion putting even more strain on family dynamics.

Adding to these stresses, Ron slipped into a state of clinical depression—a trying journey, taking him down many dark, untraversed tunnels. Because of Ron's severe exhaustion, his doctor recommended that he take three months off work and begin antidepressant medication. Arlene, too, was having health problems. She developed gangrene in her foot (a major complication from ankle surgery) and was laid up in the hospital for almost six weeks. Just after returning to her real estate career, she severely broke her right ankle, with the bone penetrating through the skin. She would undergo three more operations on the ankle, be off work for an additional ten months, and endure several months of therapy. She still suffers from ankle pain today.

Even more financial difficulties flared up. They were in a "downward spiral," as one counselor put it. They didn't have time to recover from one thing before being hit with something else. "We were physically and emotionally drained," they told me.

Then their teenager Brent, their third-born son, began to show signs of clinical depression. Brent, like Ron, was a perfectionist by nature. He was an artist with a knack for painting. Every brushstroke had to be exact. Yet no matter how beautiful his painting was, he always found something wrong with it. He was also frugal and very sensitive. He cried a lot, unable to handle the swearing and the racism he observed in the Pickering school system. "Why can't people get along?" he would ask.

Ron and Arlene decided to send Brent to the rural Bancroft high school located close to their cottage about 140 miles north. It was a smaller school with a better atmosphere, and he would stay with his grandparents. Ron and Arlene felt sure at the time they were doing the right thing, but in hindsight, they feel they missed out on three valuable years of Brent's life.

While in Bancroft, Brent met a sweet, pretty girl named Krista, who soon became the love of his life. Toward the end of his high school years, however, Brent recognized that he struggled with feelings of depression and sought help on his own from a psychiatrist. "I can handle this, Mom and Dad," he would say. For whatever reason, Brent and Krista decided to take a break in their relationship. He finished high school and started apprenticing with Ron back in Toronto, returning to Bancroft on the weekends to hang out with friends.

The day before he died, Brent was driving a forklift when he accidentally backed into and damaged a number of hollow metal steel doors. He was very distraught. This was one of the worst things that could have happened to him. Ron tried to console his son. "That's okay. My boss has insurance." But nothing cheered Brent up.

The next day, Brent awoke saying he was feeling tired. It was October 1996, approximately seven years after Vaughn's suicide. Arlene came into his room and asked if there was anything she could get him. He replied, "No. I just want to sleep in a bit more." So Arlene left, taking the other boys to school and running an errand.

Seeing Brent's truck still in the driveway at noon, Arlene was looking forward to having lunch with him. Entering the house, she heard loud music coming from the basement—out of character for Brent. She called his name. But no answer. So she went down the basement steps, quickly popped her head around the corner, didn't see him, and started back up. Her eyes had quickly scanned the dimly lit room, seeing the weights on the floor and the punching bag hanging from the ceiling. But as she started back up the stairs, she realized that what she saw wasn't the punching bag. It was Brent.

He was only twenty years old.

Unlike Vaughn, Brent left a note. It basically said that his parents were not to blame themselves or anyone else. He simply couldn't tolerate life anymore. Like Vaughn, no drugs or alcohol were found in his system—something that is unusual in suicide cases.

"WE WERE BOUND IT WASN'T GOING TO HAPPEN AGAIN"

Like a heinous, unrelenting nightmare, the heart-wrenching grief returned—and deeply intensified. Brent had displayed some signs of depression, but he would adamantly say, "I can handle this." At first, Arlene was angry with Brent that he would do such a horrible thing to her after what Vaughn had done. She was also bitter with God for allowing the death of her second son: "There will be no more praying in this house!" she lashed out at Ron. Yet she never followed through with her pronouncement, and her anger toward God dissipated when she realized her attitude and perspective were wrong.

"The stigma attached to suicide is very traumatic," Arlene said. "It's something you read about in the newspaper. It never touches your family. That would never touch a Christian family. You never think about it." Reflecting, she added, "I honestly believe people look at you differently. I didn't want to go out the door. I didn't want to look at my neighbors. I was afraid to be alone in the house. Yet, where do you go?"

Trying his best to explain what happened from a spiritual viewpoint, Ron remarked that Vaughn and Brent had "failed to understand that we are accepted in Christ." Pausing briefly, he added, "It took me a long time to understand that."

When Vaughn passed away, the shock of the tragedy changed their lives forever. Their perspective on life had changed. Yet Brent's suicide only brought more tears and more unanswered questions.

"The priorities in your life prior to something like this happening now no longer make any sense to you at all," said Arlene. "Your whole priority system shifts. And we're very aware that we have made some mistakes; some of our mistakes may have contributed to the passing of our sons." Stopping briefly, she continued, "We were bound it wasn't going to happen again."

Being referred to a Christian medical doctor who specialized in counseling was a rich blessing. Curtis and Tyler also met with him. Throughout their counseling sessions, Ron and Arlene did what every parent does when a child is lost to suicide: they asked themselves, "Where did we go wrong?"

Through the darkened sky of heartache and unanswered questions, some rays of hope shone. "After Brent passed away, we saw a real softening of Jayson. He was more open to trusting in God," Arlene shared with me as I sat before the couple in their upstairs bedroom that Sunday afternoon in November of 2002. But momentarily glancing out the window at the falling flakes of snow, she paused. The tears welled up again in her eyes and spilled over onto her cheeks.

Ron and Arlene's story wasn't finished yet. Another terrible tragedy would soon strike.

THE HAPPIEST DAY OF HIS LIFE

Their fourth-born son, Curtis, wanted more than anything to join the militia—a co-op program offered by his high school and run by the Canadian military. He was devastated when the militia told him he could not begin his training, even though he had just been accepted into the program. The program was very strict. Very regimented. And they felt that mentally, after losing two brothers, he wouldn't be stable enough to proceed with the rigorous training. Curtis bugged them, persisting, "I *want* to take this, and I'll prove myself." The militia finally agreed to let him continue—under certain conditions.

Curtis was seen by two psychologists, who gave him the green light. The Christian medical doctor who was counseling the family also agreed: "Let him do it." In spite of their recommendations, Arlene was opposed to the whole idea. "At this point, you have to understand," she said. "My world has been shaken. I've lost two children. And I'm going to put a fence around the remainder of my children." After much insistence by Curtis and the psychologists, Arlene reluctantly agreed to let her son continue in the militia.

Curtis, needless to say, was overjoyed.

The day Curtis died was probably the happiest day of his life. It was February 28, 1997—four months after Brent had passed away. There he was, standing proudly in full uniform. He had passed a major examination in the militia and was utterly thrilled to have his picture taken in his decorative attire. He had also won an award, and everything was set for his graduation from the militia that coming June. After leaving the ceremony, his parents took him out for a big submarine sandwich—his favorite meal. Arriving later that day at Ron's parents' cottage in Bancroft, Curtis was excited to show his grandparents his award. He was overjoyed!

That evening, a teenage friend who lived next door asked if Tyler and Curtis wanted to head over to an adjacent lake by snowmobile to help pile wood for an elderly lady. The two boys readily accepted the proposition. It turned out, however, that the headlight on their friend's snowmobile was broken, and the throttle cable would soon snap on Tyler's machine. Curtis's snowmobile was the only machine in working order. So now the plan was for Tyler and their teenage neighbor to travel around the lake by truck and Curtis would meet them there on the snowmobile. Ron and Arlene weren't worried. Curtis knew the lake well. And they were assured the lake was completely frozen and safe. Curtis left on his snowmobile as planned. It was 9:00 p.m. on a Friday.

Tired, Ron and Arlene went off to bed. But at 12:30 a.m. they were awakened by voices. Tyler and his friend were standing in the kitchen, somewhat upset that Curtis hadn't shown up to help pile wood. "Where's Curtis?" they asked. The question sent a chill up and down their spines.

Everyone began an anxious search. It was foggy that night, and they saw no sign of Curtis. Arlene was frantic, placing all kinds of phone calls. Ron called the police, but they just brushed him off: "It's typical of a boy his age. He's probably gone to a party somewhere."

"But that's not like Curtis," Ron insisted.

The police responded, "We can't do anything until he's been missing for twenty-four hours."

The search continued throughout the next day. By next evening the police were still somewhat uncooperative. Finally, after much pressure, the police showed up at three in the morning to take a statement.

Later that Sunday morning, Ron received a call from an elder at the local L'Amable Bible chapel where they fellowshipped. "We've cancelled our first morning service. We're going to help you look for Curtis." A short time after that call, more than eighty people stood on the cottage lawn ready to help. Taking control, the police started sending search parties several miles away. Krista, who had become good friends with Curtis after Brent's death, wanted to walk the lake. But the police told her not to waste her time and pointed her elsewhere. Ignoring them, Krista started walking around the frozen perimeter. Greg, now eight years old, wanted to go too, but was delayed.

It wasn't long after that when they heard Krista's scream. Close friends of Ron and Arlene's, also up for the weekend, ran off across the ice. There was chatter coming across the walkie-talkies, but the ambulance crew, standing near the cottage, were not moving—even though they had a sled ready and waiting. Looking across the lake, Arlene knew the worst.

Krista found Curtis that Sunday at 10:30 a.m. Apparently, in the dense fog Friday evening, Curtis had gone off course and didn't see the shore until it was too late. There were skid marks in the snow where he hit the brakes at the last moment—but he died instantly when his snowmobile and his body hit the rocks and trees on the shore. Curtis was seventeen years old.

Tyler, the next oldest brother, who considered Curtis his best friend, was distraught and wracked with guilt. "Why didn't I go with him? Maybe I could have seen the rock before he did." Jayson, who had started to soften after Brent's death, was now bitterly angry again with God. *Why would God let this happen?* Standing on the ice, Jayson was screaming and swearing at God. Jayson later shared with me that everything that day was a blur. The only thing he really remembers is feeling very confused.

His grandmother, Marion, remarked to me, "I cannot look out the window and across the lake without thinking of Curtis."

Every time I pass those darkened rocks by boat or on foot, I, too, am reminded of Curtis's tragic death.

FINISHING VICTORIOUS

In a span of less than eight years, Ron and Arlene had buried three young sons. Jayson, Tyler, and Greg had buried three brothers. My heart grieved for them. I wondered why God would allow something as horrible as this to happen. And I wondered how Ron, Arlene, and their family could survive such incredible pain. A Christian woman opened up to Arlene: "I've lost a mother. I've lost a husband. But how traumatic it must be to lose a child." Most parents have not lost one young son—let alone three. Arlene personally shared with me the storms she fought in the grieving process: "At times like this you're physically and emotionally tired. You're drained. You're exhausted. You want to read. You want to understand. You want to pray. And there are times you can't because you are empty; there is nothing left. You can't shed another tear. There's nothing more. You're numb."

Ron also shared, "Not a day goes by that I don't have some sort of a twinge inside that I miss the boys. And some days it's very, very heavy. A whole lot more than just a twinge. And I'm really hurting inside. It almost feels like my heart is dripping. It feels like I am leaking inside, I am just so hurting."

Looking ahead, Arlene vowed, "We have to go on. We have to maintain some stability in our home." She added, "It's hard as a parent. You have a responsibility to help your children get through this when you don't know how to get through it yourself."

The two-and-a-half-hour drive back home that November night from Ron and Arlene's place gave me a chance to clear my mind and reflect on the day's interview. Driving north through the falling snow on the tranquil, darkened highway, the thought struck me: *In many ways, Ron and Arlene's family, prior to the tragedies, was your typical Christian home. In fact, in certain aspects it was far better.*

No family, understandably, is perfect. Ron and Arlene, like many young couples, struggled early on with finances, work commitments, church responsibilities, their marriage relationship, and their children's early illnesses. All things said, this was not a chaotic, unloving, and dysfunctional family. For the most part, the kids were happy and all the family members enjoyed close relationships with one another. They attended church together. As a leader in the church, Ron even had the privilege of baptizing all six of his sons.

I had a long one-on-one conversation with Tyler at the Bible college he was attending. Toward the end of the evening, I hesitated, wondering if I should ask the next question. Even though I was pretty sure of what Tyler's response would be, I knew it was a very sensitive matter to broach. Looking into his face, I asked, "Tyler, do you in any way blame your parents for your brothers' suicides?" Without hesitating, he answered emphatically, "Not at all. Not at all. I think my parents have done an excellent job in raising us. It's not something they could have prevented."

As Arlene attested, a stigma is certainly attached to suicide. Families receive as much finger-pointing as sympathy. Most parents believe that something as horrible as suicide could never happen in their family. But the truth is, it can. The tragedies that struck Ron and Arlene's family could have struck any Christian family.

Moreover, it's rather easy for us to condemn individuals for becoming indifferent toward God in the face of a tragedy. We get so comfortable and smug as "armchair Christians," reclining on our faith and coolly saying to someone hurting, "Just trust God and everything will be okay." Had you or I, however, experienced the tragic loss of three children or three siblings, would we have turned to God? If I had lost my brother to suicide, and maybe my sister in a snowmobile accident, would I be where I am today? Would my faith have survived the onslaught of unanswerable questions arising from my deepest sorrow?

I can't answer these questions.

I think all of us, searching deep inside our hearts, would have to confess that it is only by the grace of God that we are where we are today. We must not act as the jury, judge, and executioner in condemning our fellow Christians for losing faith when the same tragedy, and the same after-effects to our faith, could have easily come upon us.

Why does God allow us to suffer? And where is God in our deepest hurt? Ron and Arlene didn't ask me these tough questions while I was in their home. But if they had, how would I have responded? What would I say to Arlene, who suffered years of childhood sexual abuse, incapacitating foot pain, and the tragic loss of three dear sons? What would I say to Ron, who struggled with depression and suffered the heartrending loss of three beloved sons? What would I say to Greg, who lost three older brothers and will have to battle celiac disease the rest of his life? What words would I have for Tyler, who also lost three brothers, one of whom he considered his best friend? And what would I say to Jayson, who cannot celebrate his birthday without remembering that it was the day they buried his closest brother Vaughn?

Where is God in our suffering?

The chapters to come will be, without a doubt, the most difficult material I have ever written. Entire books have been published on this daunting subject. Brilliant men and women of God have spent countless hours trying to dig through the mystery surrounding the issue of suffering. To think that we can fully answer all these towering questions in three or four chapters is ludicrous. Yet I believe a couple of closing illustrations will be of tremendous help to you in better understanding God in the complex area of suffering.

To some degree, the remaining chapters will summarize and assemble almost all of the insights we've gleaned so far on our journey. This is the place where our diligent digging into God's Word will really pay off. This is where we bring together all the "stepping-stones" we've unearthed in the previous three books and try to arrange them into a meaningful path. We will also see in the following chapters what happened when Ron and Arlene arranged their own stepping-stones in an attempt to break through the storms of heartache, guilt, and shame.

I would strongly encourage you to read, reread, and meditate on the truths presented in the following pages. This leg of our quest will be extremely difficult, challenging, and soul-searching; but if we can keep our focus squarely on God, I fervently believe we will finish this part of the journey victorious!

WHY DOES GOD ALLOW SUFFERING?

*It is the spectators, the people who
are outside, looking at the tragedy, from
whose ranks the skeptics come; it is not those
who are actually in the arena and who
know suffering from the inside. Indeed,
the fact is that it is the world's greatest
sufferers who have produced the most
shining examples of unconquerable faith.*[1]

—JAMES S. STEWART

4

"YOU HAVE A LOT OF
EXPLAINING TO DO, GOD!"

James S. Stewart, a Scottish theologian, is correct when he suggests that most skeptics of God's existence are armchair spectators who have endured very little suffering in their lifetimes. Oh sure, the skeptic can turn on CNN any evening to find all the evidence he or she needs to prove that we live on a violent, hateful, and chaotic planet. And the agnostic or atheist can use this evidence if he or she so desires as ammunition against the existence of a supreme being. But most critics remain mere spectators—not active or even passive participants in the stadium of suffering.

In contrast, loyal heroes of faith down through the ages who *have* faced unimaginable adversity head-on in the arena of affliction are often the ones who understand best the power, the rewards, and the reasons we suffer. For these faith heroes, suffering, rather than evidence *against* the existence of God, becomes evidence *for* the wisdom, the mercy, the caring, and the grace of our loving Creator and Lord.

WHY DOES GOD ALLOW SUFFERING?

What possible evidence—or reasons—might God offer to explain why we suffer? Let's quickly deal with the two that make the most sense—from our perspective anyway.

First, believers and nonbelievers alike will usually agree that a good deal of our suffering is *our fault.* Now, when I say, "our fault," I don't necessarily mean our own personal fault, but rather the fault of the human race in general. A troubled Jewish scholar challenged Elie Wiesel, a survivor of the holocaust, one day: "How can you tell us to continue to believe in God after Auschwitz?" To which Elie dramatically replied, "My friend, I think the question after Auschwitz is not how we can believe in God but how can we believe in man."[2]

Many religious teachers and philosophers will agree that mankind is to blame for a host of evils inflicted and perpetuated on our world: wars, terrorism, racism, murder, abortion, rape, drug abuse, child prostitution, kidnapping, greed, hate, selfishness, and broken homes. "They sow the wind and reap the whirlwind," we read in Hosea 8:7. C. S. Lewis and Dr. Charles Stanley estimate that approximately 60–80 percent of the adversity we face in life has been caused directly by our own sin and foolishness—or indirectly by the sin and foolishness of someone else.[3] Sometimes the trials we face are "acts of God," but often we create the trials and acts ourselves and then blame the Almighty.

The second obvious reason believers suffer has to do with the universal conflict between good and evil. It only makes sense that if we're fighting a spiritual battle against the powers of evil we're going to get ambushed and assailed (see Eph. 6:12–18). "This is spiritual warfare, not a tea party," says Dr. John MacArthur.[4] If we're fighting the demons while serving on the front lines of God's elite army, we're going to get ambushed. It's inevitable. And we're very likely going to suffer some serious wounds on the battlefield—be they spiritual, emotional, or physical. Fighting and suffering for the sake of Christ should be counted a rich privilege (see Phil. 1:29 NLT).

I received an e-mail recently from a missionary father whose daughter was leaving Canada to fly to Pakistan to teach children in a missionary role. The father was delighted with his daughter's decision.

But after distributing this good news, he heard from several people who forwarded e-mails about Christians who were being horribly persecuted over there, trying to get it through to this father just how much violence, kidnapping, and killing was going on inside Pakistan's borders.

The father became angry and wrote in response, "What do you suppose God thinks when He calls believers into ministry, places them in proximity to the unsaved, brings them into contact so they can be a witness?" Of course it's dangerous! What did these friends expect? If it's God's sovereign will that you spread the gospel to the unsaved in perilous countries like Pakistan, Saudi Arabia, Sudan, and China, you *will* be in real danger, and you *will* be persecuted in some way—perhaps even losing your life.

Today we have teenagers and youngsters running around the church sporting wristbands and necklaces with the acronym, WWJD (What Would Jesus Do?). Well, *what would Jesus do?* Jesus suffered as he spread the gospel, didn't he? Wasn't it Jesus who said, "And anyone who does not carry his cross and follow me cannot be my disciple" (Luke 14:27)? Didn't Peter write, "This suffering is all part of what God has called you to. Christ, who suffered for you, is your example. Follow in his steps" (1 Peter 2:21 NLT)? Ironically, some churches selling this WWJD merchandise in their bookstores are the same churches teaching youth from the pulpit that it is not God's will that you suffer. What a gross contradiction! As Spurgeon said, "There are no crownwearers in Heaven that were not crossbearers here below."[5]

Having examined the understandable, let's move on to the part of suffering that is the hardest to understand.

Does God really have a lot of explaining to do?

DRIVING US CLOSER

Very few Christians in North America have not heard of Steven Curtis Chapman—or at least been touched in some way by his inspiring music. Perhaps one of the most celebrated contemporary

Christian artists of all time, Steven has sold millions of albums, had forty-one number one radio hits, and accumulated four Grammy Awards, forty-seven Dove Awards, and an American Music Award so far in his music career.

But in the first couple of years of the new millennium, Steven faced the "lightning, thunder, and storm winds" he wrote about on his album *Declaration.* Actually, the waves of suffering came crashing down soon after he had finished his previous album, *Speechless,* in 1999. Steven mourned alongside grieving friends who had lost their child to cancer. Another family, close to the Chapmans, with four young children, lost their mother in a tragic horseback-riding accident. Steven, with his wife Mary Beth, looked on as two young families struggled to cope with their adopted children's Reactive Attachment Disorder (a trying psychiatric illness more common in adopted kids who have been previously abused).

Soon after beginning his next album, *Declaration,* Steven found himself wrestling "with words to communicate the depth of God's grace."[6] He also found himself struggling to cope with his mother's diagnosed stage-three cancer. Temporarily halting work on the album, Steven took time to be by his mom's side.

Then another huge wave came crashing down—one of the most feared waves for a professional singer. Approaching the completion of the album, Steven found himself unable to reach every high note on the background vocals. Instantly his singing voice was gone. Visiting the Vanderbilt Voice Clinic in Nashville, he discovered that he had a paralyzed vocal cord. His voice would probably return, but it would take six to eight months. Even then, there was no guarantee.

Fortunately, Steven had finished the lead tracks and the album was eventually completed. One of the songs Steven wrote on the album was titled "Bring It On." Read the lyrics carefully:

> I didn't come lookin' for trouble
>
> And I don't want to fight needlessly
>
> But I'm not gonna hide in a bubble

YOU HAVE A LOT OF EXPLAINING TO DO

If trouble comes for me
I can feel my heart beating faster
I can tell something's coming down
But if it's gonna make me grow stronger then ...

Bring it on
Let the lightning flash, let the thunder roll, let the
    storm winds blow
Bring it on
Let the trouble come, let the hard rain fall, let it make
    me strong
Bring it on

Now, maybe you're thinkin' I'm crazy
And maybe I need to explain some things
'Cause I know I've got an enemy waiting
Who wants to bring me pain
But what he never seems to remember
What he means for evil God works for good
So I will not retreat or surrender

Now, I don't want to sound like some hero
'Cause it's God alone that my hope is in
But I'm not gonna run from the very things
That would drive me closer to Him
So bring it on.[7]

To Steven, his lyrics had sprung to life overnight—*his life.* He had requested God to "bring it on," to bring on trials in his life if it would make him a stronger Christian and drive him closer to his heavenly Father. And God, answering Steven's bold request, did indeed "bring it on." In Steven's life, the lightning flashed, the thunder rolled, and the storm winds blew. The question was, would his faith survive the relentless pounding?

The "gift of music," said Steven, is "a gift I often use to block out pain and confusion."[8] However, that God-given gift had suddenly vanished. When he lost his singing voice, he lost a valuable aid that had helped him deal with tragedies such as the school shootings in Paducah and Columbine. When he turned to the Bible, he realized that his understanding of God's character didn't exactly mesh with how God described himself in his Word. In an interview with *CCM* magazine, Steven confessed,

> I would run to God's Word for comfort and answers, and feel more alienated by it than drawn to him. I would open up my Bible and think, "I've never seen *that* before. *That* doesn't sound like you. I thought I knew you."[9]

Like so many suffering saints, Steven discovered that often when our world is turned upside down, so is our understanding of God. Our pain often drives us to God's Word for answers. Our suffering frequently turns our focus toward the Father's heart. And when our focus is redirected, quite often we gain a fresh understanding of our almighty Lord.

Complete surrender of the will is the starting point to living a Christ-like life (see Mark 8:34). In his popular book *The Problem of Pain*, C. S. Lewis wrote, "The human spirit will not even begin to try to surrender self-will as long as all seems to be well with it."[10] All too often, pleasure cheers on the champion of self-will in the "me stadium," while God, standing patiently outside, is denied admittance to the "sold out" event. To gain a top-down perspective on life we must relinquish our self-will—our self-centered resolve to be the center of our universe. And nothing routs out self-will like the instrument of pain.

Trials and adversities often do what bliss and ecstasy cannot. "We can rest contentedly in our sins and in our stupidities," says C. S. Lewis; and we can take pleasure for granted. "But pain insists upon being attended to. God whispers to us in our pleasures, speaks in our conscience, but shouts in our pains: it is His megaphone to rouse a deaf world."[11]

Best-selling author and painter Joni Eareckson Tada, whose daily radio program received the "Radio Program of the Year" award from the National Religious Broadcasters, has been in a wheelchair now as a quadriplegic for more than thirty-seven years. She said this to Larry King recently on national television:

> I think suffering is God's way of sometimes waking us up out of our spiritual slumber with an ice-cold splash in the face and getting us seriously to consider his claims, who He is and where we're going.[12]

Sometimes God wishes to "wake us up" or have a little "chat" with us. He offers us eternal riches, but often our hearts are already filled with the world's distractions and "clutter" (see Luke 14:33). "We 'have all we want' is a terrible saying when 'all' does not include God," writes C. S. Lewis. "We find God an interruption."[13]

When all is going well in our "me stadiums," we feel we don't need God. Tragically, God is deemed only as a spectator at best—more like an "interruption," as Lewis puts it. Why bust myself trying to develop an intimate relationship with God if this relationship will not help me collect more "stuff" here on earth? (See Matt. 19:16–24.) In our deepest pain, God's Word penetrates past the world's distractions to the core of our hearts. It is then that a whole new world is opened up to us.

But for some saints, suffering is like grease smeared on their nearsighted eyeglasses; it only further clouds their vision of God and makes them angrier. It happens. Many saints, when hit with adversity, start feeling sorry for themselves, adopting a destructive "woe is me" attitude. And perhaps the scariest thing is that it's almost impossible (from our perspective anyway) to predict who will be driven *to* God and who will be driven *away* from God by tragedy. Nevertheless, the majority of saints find that God, by his loving grace, empowers us to remove these greasesmeared, nearsighted glasses, allowing us to catch a clear glimpse of life from his perspective (see Job 42:5).

WHY DOES GOD ALLOW SUFFERING?

Philip Yancey points out in his best-selling book *Disappointment with God* that, in the end, Job praised God from the ashes well before God gave him back double what he lost. "Only one thing had changed," said Yancey. "God had given Job a glimpse of the big picture."[14]

To see the big picture in our suffering is actually to see nothing at all. That's right: The big picture is invisible from the world's vantage point. Only those with the glasses of faith can spot some of the major interlocking pieces in God's eternal portrait.

Paul writes:

> For our light and momentary troubles are achieving for us an eternal glory that far outweighs them all. So we fix our eyes not on what is seen, but on what is unseen. For what is seen is temporary, but what is unseen is eternal. (2 Cor. 4:17–18)

The death of a beloved child, a painful divorce, a debilitating illness, or the loss of a job forces us to trade our horizontal perspective on life for a truly divine perspective. It allows us to see much more clearly the big picture—what's important in life and what isn't. Suddenly, our priorities do a 180. All of a sudden, what was important before, we now label "trivial." That big promotion we've been gunning for, that new international business account we've been hoping to land, that new car or home we've been dreaming about—suddenly, none of that matters anymore. My friend Andrew, whose heart was broken and his bank account emptied after his wife walked out on him, said he wouldn't wish what happened to him on his worst enemy. He used to think, "God, how could you do this to me?" But now his attitude has changed: "God, how could you *not* do this to me? How could you not bring about this trial knowing how much good would come out of it?" For it was through Andrew's deepest suffering that he was drawn closer to God.

Toward the end of her interview with Larry King, Joni Eareckson Tada shared this beautiful thought from her heart:

> I hope I can take this wheelchair to Heaven with me. I know … that's not biblically correct.… But if I could, I would take it with me and I would be standing next to my

savior Jesus Christ, and I would say, "Lord, do you see this wheelchair? Well, before you send it to hell, I want to tell you something about it. You were right, when you said, in this world we would have trouble. And there's a lot of trouble being a quadriplegic, but you know what, the weaker I was in that thing, the harder I leaned on you and the harder I leaned on you, the stronger I discovered you to be. Thank you for the bruising of a blessing it was, this severe mercy. Thank you."[15]

Yet many in the charismatic movement don't share Joni's attitude. Many would want us to believe that God's first desire is for us to have a trouble-free, prosperous, and healthy life—and that it is the Devil who wants us to go through trials of spinal cord paralysis or live in poverty.

Actually, it's almost the opposite. It's *the Devil* who wants all believers to be incredibly rich and live a pain-free life so that we will forget about God. Pastors who work closely with famous athletes and other celebrities will tell you the same thing: Individuals with the biggest salaries, the best health, the nicest mansions, the greatest popularity, and the most beautiful spouses are usually the ones who want very little or nothing to do with God. They've attained it all themselves in the "me stadium." So where's the need for the Almighty?

The reason more believers don't win the lottery, land multimillion dollar contracts, and inherit huge family fortunes is that God usually won't allow the Devil the opportunity to attack us in these ways. God doesn't want you to become so rich that you forget him. One of God's biggest priorities is to keep you humble so that you will always realize your need of him. Having said that, God sometimes blesses his children with great wealth—yet with the material riches he often provides something very important: *godly wisdom to keep his child close to the Father's heart.*

Listen to the wisdom writer's request to God:

> Keep falsehood and lies far from me; give me neither poverty nor riches, but give me only my daily bread.

WHY DOES GOD ALLOW SUFFERING?

> Otherwise, I may have too much and disown you and say,
> 'Who is the LORD?' Or I may become poor and steal, and
> so dishonor the name of my God. (Prov. 30:8–9)

Go into life with this attitude and prayer, and God might do just the opposite: He might actually bless you with more material wealth than you ever imagined. Then again he might not. Pain and hurt humble us just enough so that we can spot the rich facets of our heavenly Father's character (see Job 42:5–6). God's grace and faithfulness in times of great need come alive to us in magnificent texture and context. And through our pain and our tears, we are humbled and driven into the arms of God (see 2 Cor. 12:8–10). *God uses suffering to refine us!* It is impossible for us to wrap our arms tightly around God while our arms are wrapped tightly around the world's "stuff." Indeed, "Temporary suffering is a small price to pay for eternal happiness."[16]

> In this you greatly rejoice, though now for a little while you
> may have had to suffer grief in all kinds of trials. These
> have come so that your faith—of greater worth than gold,
> which perishes even though refined by fire—may be
> proved genuine and may result in praise, glory and honor
> when Jesus Christ is revealed. (1 Peter 1:6–7)

REFINED FOR GOD'S GLORY

Dr. Charles Stanley insists, "The reason so many of us struggle so intensely with adversity is that we have yet to adopt God's perspective and priorities."[17] If we could only see the eternal rewards of our pain and suffering, I think we would view adversity in a whole different light.

When I asked how their relationship with God had changed as a result of the storms in their life, including the deaths of their three sons, Ron replied, "First of all, it humbled me. It certainly got me to my knees. It has strengthened my faith in God. For me, Christianity has become more real, rather than just textbook style. It has become three-dimensional—dynamic, alive!"

Arlene shared that in her darkest moments, she found that: "You want to read. You want to understand. You want to pray. And there are times you can't because you are empty. There's nothing left. You can't shed another tear." Arlene said also that her suffering has resulted in a faith that is much more dynamic.

Hudson Taylor, pioneer missionary to China, while suffering terribly in the last few days of his life, turned to his wife and said, "I cannot read; I cannot pray; I can scarcely think, but," and then he managed a smile, "I can trust!"[18] Arlene, like Ron, admitted that the deaths of her sons was very humbling, bringing her to the realization of just how much more she needed to rely on and trust in God. At the height of our suffering, often trust is the only thing we can do—or at least strive to do.

Tyler and Greg echoed their parents' thoughts. Greg, the youngest son, in the tenth grade at the time of my interview, said, "Overall, it has made me stronger and made me rely more on God. At first I was a little bitter, but my life changed for the better." After enduring one heinous tragedy after another for almost a decade, Ron, Arlene, and their sons have had their spiritual lives beautifully refined for God's greatest glory. Often it is those who suffer the most who expect God to explain the least.

When Steven Curtis Chapman finally recovered his voice, he gained a whole new perspective on this invaluable refining process. While mostly lip-synching a song on a last-minute video shoot on a San Francisco beach, Steven found himself hitting notes he hadn't reached in nearly three months. "It dawned on me, 'Wait a minute. You just sang a note you couldn't sing yesterday!'"[19] His singing voice had returned!

Through his "silent nights," Steven's faith has been buffeted. He has cried out from the pit of despair and bewilderment. He has been forced to take a second look at the puzzle of suffering. And his walk with God will never be the same. Steven continues to sing forth the praises of God.

WHY DOES GOD ALLOW SUFFERING?

Steven says,

> Through this, I have learned that we can control where we allow things that we can't understand to fall. They either fall between us and God and we become angry. Or we allow these things to fall outside of us and press us in closer to God.[20]

Without a doubt, God provides all the grace we need to press us closer to him and survive any onslaught of suffering:

> And the God of all grace, who called you to his eternal glory in Christ, after you have suffered a little while, will himself restore you and make you strong, firm and steadfast. To him be the power for ever and ever. Amen. (1 Peter 5:10–11)

No Need to Explain

We've already uncovered one major benefit that comes about from our afflictions. All suffering, no matter what its origin may be, really, really hurts. And often it is this hurt that greatly tests our faith, while at the same time, driving us into the arms of God to produce an even more intimate and rewarding relationship with our heavenly Father. Joni Eareckson Tada says, after thirty-seven difficult years in a wheelchair, "I would really rather be in this chair knowing Him, than on my feet without Him."[21]

But even more rewards are associated with suffering.

Ron, Arlene, and their family related several other good things that came out of the boys' deaths. A young girl came to visit Ron and Arlene one day. She said that Vaughn's death had caused her to stop and think about eternal issues. As a result, she came to a saving knowledge of Jesus Christ. Because of the suicide, this girl will spend eternity in heaven where she will see Vaughn once again. (Even suicide cannot pluck a true believer out of God's hand. See John 10:29; Rom. 8:38–39; Eph. 1:13–14.)[22]

Vaughn's death also triggered a neighbor to seriously evaluate her spiritual condition. She told Arlene one day that she kept watching for the family to collapse, thinking they would just give up their faith completely. Instead, she was deeply influenced by how well the family coped with the loss of the boys. And she began to think that maybe there really was something to this Christianity after all. Dr. Charles Stanley reminds us, "Nothing gets the attention of an unbeliever like a saint who is suffering successfully."[23]

Another woman in her fifties, who knew the family well, broke down in tears after Vaughn's death. Her beloved husband had died seven years earlier of cancer, but as far as anyone knew she had never shed a tear. Vaughn's passing away triggered the therapeutic grieving process for her.

A middle-aged couple, also suffering hardships of their own, approached Ron and Arlene one day. The man said, "You two were a real encouragement to me. You really helped me through my life." Ron and Arlene's family have been a true inspiration to many hurting Christians. They've received calls in the middle of the night from other grieving parents who have also lost children and wanted to know how Ron and Arlene got through their roughest waters of despair (see 2 Cor. 1:3–5).

In addition, all three funerals were widely attended by family and friends, including teenagers. Hundreds of receptive unbelievers heard the gospel message because of the deaths of Vaughn, Brent, and Curtis. The lives of many, from every walk of life, have been affected for the better. Even Jayson, who had difficulty seeing any good come from Curtis's accidental death, admitted that someone was likely deeply touched from it in a life-transforming way. The family agreed that if even one person was saved as a result of the deaths, then they could see some meaning to it all. To this day, however, no one knows for certain the true spiritual wake these three boys left behind when they passed on into heaven.

In God's providence, he certainly does work good out of evil; it is his exclusive trademark and one of his greatest accomplishments. Christ's gruesome death on the cross is all the evidence we need.

WHY DOES GOD ALLOW SUFFERING?

Dr. Stanley says,

> We must remember that Christ's death, burial, and resurrection serve as the context of all our suffering. God, through those events, took the greatest tragedy in the history of the world and used it to accomplish His greatest triumph—the salvation of man. If the murder of the perfect Son of God can be explained, how much more can we trust that God is accomplishing His purposes through the adversity we face every day?[24]

If God can supply a rational explanation for why he allowed his perfect and only begotten Son to be grotesquely crucified on a cross, does he really need to explain to us exactly why it is that we are suffering? Should we not accept, by faith, that if our heavenly Father had a good reason for allowing his only Son to be cruelly murdered, that he must also have a good reason for allowing us to suffer the pain and adversity we do?

Considering that it was *our* sins that sent Christ to the cross in the first place, and that it is *our* hidden sins that break our heavenly Father's heart every day, maybe it is we—and not God—who have a lot of explaining to do.

OFTEN IT IS THIS HURT
THAT GREATLY TESTS OUR
FAITH, WHILE AT THE
SAME TIME, DRIVING US
INTO THE ARMS OF GOD
TO PRODUCE AN EVEN
MORE INTIMATE AND
REWARDING RELATIONSHIP
WITH OUR HEAVENLY
FATHER.

WHY DOES GOD ALLOW SUFFERING?

*Surely I spoke of things I did not
understand, things too wonderful for me
to know.... My ears had heard of
you but now my eyes have seen you.*

—JOB 42:3, 5

5
IS GOD PUNISHING ME?

God can resurrect much good out of tragedy. In his book of Bible lists, H. L. Willmington lists twenty-five reasons why Christians suffer, which includes the following:

- To show God's sovereignty (Gen. 45:5–8; 50:20)
- To give us insight into God's nature (Job 42:5)
- To further the gospel witness (Acts 8:1–5; 16:25–34)
- To reveal ourselves to ourselves (Luke 15:18)
- To produce the fruit of patience (James 1:3–4)
- To produce the fruit of joy (Ps. 30:5; 126:5–6)
- To make us like Christ (1 Peter 4:12–13)
- To Glorify God (John 9:1–3)

Willmington rightly includes another reason why Christians suffer: To chasten us for our sin (see 1 Peter 4:17; Heb. 12:5–6).[1]

WHY DOES GOD ALLOW SUFFERING?

Now, it might unnerve us to think that the adversity we're suffering might be God's way of directly punishing us for our sins. But who can forget the scandalous story of David—Israel's greatest king, who cried out to God for mercy and forgiveness for his sins of adultery with Bathsheba and the murder of her husband? According to Mosaic law, David deserved the death penalty (see Ex. 21:12; Lev. 20:10). But David's genuine repentance ultimately saved him (see Ps. 51). God certainly did have mercy and forgave David completely. But God also told David that because David had struck down Uriah with the sword, "the sword will never depart from your house" (2 Sam. 12:10).

David's first son with Bathsheba died shortly after birth. David's other son, Absalom, slept with some of David's wives and tried to hunt his father and kill him. Another son, Amnon, cunningly lured his virgin half sister Tamar into his room and raped her. Absalom, furious, retaliated by having his servants murder his brother Amnon. And through it all, David's kingdom was split. Israel's greatest earthly king was forgiven all right, but the horrible consequences of his actions hounded him and his family the rest of their lives.

Think back to all the time-outs you received in your younger years. How many times did your parents need to explain to you *exactly why* you were punished? Does God need to explain each and every time he disciplines us for our ungodly actions? Are we not mature enough in our faith to figure it all out for ourselves?

If God really is disciplining us for a specific sin, then he will somehow make that very plain to us. If we're wracking our brains wondering why God might be punishing us, then he's probably not punishing us. Discipline and punishment are meaningless if the perpetrator cannot see any connection to the crime.

Even spiritual leaders have trouble grasping this truth. A thirty-three-year-old Baptist pastor and his wife asked of God, "Why us? Are we being punished?" after their daughter was diagnosed in the womb with the birth defect of spina bifida.[2]

Arlene, too, initially felt that God was punishing her and Ron with the death of their oldest son, Vaughn. She thought this was God's chastisement for their sin of premarital sex. For years she felt this way … but not anymore. One day the thought struck her, "Why would God wait eighteen years to take the life of our teenage son? It doesn't make any sense. This isn't how my heavenly Father operates."

The Bible makes it clear that God will discipline those he loves. (All one has to do is study the life of David to grasp this truth.) But as I've stated elsewhere in this book series, I don't see, in our modern times, a significant, observable link in general between the specific sins we commit and the adversity we suffer. Admittedly, promiscuous sex, alcohol, smoking, illegal drugs, and gambling do take their toll on our health—and on our families. But take an honest look around and you'll notice that many godly believers are suffering greatly, while many loose-living believers and unbelievers are just floating through life carefree. In Scripture, the wisdom writer confesses, "In this meaningless life of mine I have seen both of these: a righteous man perishing in his righteousness, and a wicked man living long in his wickedness" (Eccl. 7:15).

Why does the degree and amount of unpreventable suffering seem to have very little correlation with how godly one is? I have no way to explain why the link between our sin and God's discipline seems less apparent today than it did in Old Testament times. Some might suggest it's because of God's patience and the fact that we're living in God's parenting strategy of grace. Sometimes we do create the trials and tragedies ourselves. But most of the suffering we experience in life is not the result of God directly punishing us for some specific sin we committed. God will not wait five, ten, or eighteen years to punish us for a particular sin and then leave us wondering in our anguish, "What was that all about?"

WRONG ANSWERS FROM RIGHT MOTIVES

Well-meaning folk frequently try to come up with pat answers for people who are suffering deeply. Often though, serene silence, a caring hug, earnest prayers, and a warm dinner delivered to the home are the best gifts anyone could give. Telling someone "God is punishing you" *is definitely the wrong answer.* Most of the time God isn't punishing us for a specific sin—and furthermore, you don't know God's mind.

Here are three other *wrong responses* commonly offered to grieving people:

- **WRONG RESPONSE NUMBER ONE:** *God took your loved one home early because he couldn't wait any longer to enjoy his or her presence in heaven.* An angry fifteen-year-old girl, Jesse, whose eleven-year-old sister died because of a medical mistake made by the doctors and nurses, said this: "I don't believe in God anymore. People keep telling me that God took her—God needed her—when we needed her."[3]

  Remember we discovered that God, being our eternal and transcendent Creator, is everywhere along our timeline. Therefore, from the Almighty's perspective, a genuine believer is already in heaven, and the Lord is already enjoying his or her presence and worship. Moreover, the Holy Spirit already indwells you if you are a genuine believer. Positionally, we as true children of God are already in heaven (see Eph. 1:20; 2:6).

- **WRONG RESPONSE NUMBER TWO:** *God, looking into the future, could see the pain and suffering your loved one would go through in life and decided to spare him or her from it.* (I guess you could term this line of thinking "divine euthanasia.") Someone thoughtlessly provided this answer to Edward Kuhlman when his sixteen-year-old son died of cancer. Dr. Kuhlman responded, "Why was he born at all?"[4] Elsewhere in this book series we learned that every facet of our lives has been carefully handcrafted by God to bring him maximum glory in the big picture of life. God doesn't say, "Oops! I made a boo-boo! I think it would be better if I cut short this life early to save him from what's coming." *God never has a plan B!*

- **WRONG RESPONSE NUMBER THREE:** *God had to use this suffering to bring about good.* One pastor, Dr. Jim Conway, recounted the intense siege of suffering he endured when his sixteen-year-old daughter Becki had her leg amputated because of a malignancy—despite twenty-four-hour prayer vigils and thousands of praying believers. As the pastor was leaving a restaurant a few days later, a man grasped his coat and said, "Jim, I think God has allowed this to happen because it has brought about a revival in our church." Dr. Conway responded, "So what is God going to do to bring another revival when this one passes, chop off Becki's other leg? Then her arm and her other arm? There isn't enough of Becki to keep any church spiritually alive, if that is what it takes."[5]

    This last "wrong answer" that was supplied to Dr. Conway highlights a common misunderstanding. Most books on suffering stop here and never closely examine, explain, or illustrate the root cause of our suffering. The principal cause of each individual case of suffering does not arise from God's need to produce some good from our point of view. In fact, we read in Romans 2:4 of how God will use kindness to lead us to repentance.

Often those who suffer the most are the most adamant that God is allowing these trials *solely* because he needs to bring about some good in their immediate situation. Often it is the die-hard saints who steadfastly insist God has allowed their suffering solely to strengthen their faith. To think that the Almighty may not have a good reason for allowing us to go through the torrents of pain and adversity would make us cringe and cower.

Now please, don't get me wrong here. God often does, from our perspective, bring about much good from our tragedies, as we've already discovered. And God does have a good reason for allowing us to suffer. But that good reason is not in the small picture of everyday life events, but in the big picture of God's overall plan in the universe.

Let me explain by showing you the small picture and the big picture in Job's life.

GOD'S PICTURE GALLERY

Why exactly did Job suffer? Well, many would argue it was to increase and strengthen his faith (the small picture). True, Job gained insight into God's character that he never had before. "Surely I spoke of things I did not understand," Job cried out to God, "things too wonderful for me to know.... My ears had heard of you but now my eyes have seen you" (Job 42:3, 5).

Yet Job was already one of the most—if not *the* most—innocent, upright, and godly men of his day. Would God totally destroy Job, snatching away all his possessions and killing his seven sons and three daughters, all in an attempt to increase Job's faith and insight by what—maybe 15 or 20 percent? (Did gaining back twice the possessions he lost justify the bitter agony Job endured?) If this were God's primary reason for allowing Job to suffer horrendously, why isn't God doing it to many other saints today? If God thought it wise to devastate Job for his good, why not totally devastate the rest of believers by allowing Satan to bankrupt us and kill all our sons and daughters—all within the span of only a couple minutes?[6]

God had another, much grander goal in mind than just increasing Job's faith. One reason God allowed this series of tragedies was to use Job's harrowing story to impress upon the hearts of hundreds of millions of suffering believers who would later read of Job's horrific experiences this very important truth: *No matter what happens in life, God is the altogether sovereign ruler of the universe who is in complete control at all times.* No matter how much affliction we face, God is our fair, righteous, and loving heavenly Father who does all that he pleases for his greatest glory. Using Job's story to help other hurting believers was still in the small picture from God's perspective. God, however, never told Job of his behind-the-scenes purpose. From Job's perspective, his suffering made no sense at all. (I'll explain shortly the reason Job suffered in the big picture.)

Again, to better understand God, we *must* break past the entrenched mind-set held by many believers that absolutely *all* suffering is for *our* immediate good. You might disagree with me, quoting Romans 8:28: "And we know that in all things God works for the good of those who love him, who have been called according to his purpose." Isn't this proof that whatever happens, no matter how awful it may be, is really for *our good?*

To interpret this verse accurately we must look at the context surrounding Romans 8:28—and the Scriptures as a whole. "The best manuscript evidence records this verse as, 'we know that God causes all things …' good."[7] There is no sense of *immediate* good suggested in the verse. What is the "good" that God brings about? This verse, in the restricted context, is most likely referring to the believer's sanctification (practical purity). Paul is saying that in trouble, hardship, persecution, famine, nakedness, danger, or sword (see v. 35) we are being conformed into the likeness of Christ. That is the good spoken of here. Of course, some believers become cold toward God when ambushed by suffering, and they never return to the intimacy they once enjoyed.

Where is the good here?

Recently I was visiting a large church in Ontario, Canada where the preacher said this regarding our suffering: "God always has our best interests in mind." After the service I made my way toward the front and waited until others had finished introducing themselves and asking their questions. Then I shook hands with the preacher, introduced myself, and asked, "Do you mind if I ask you a question?"

"Not at all," he replied.

"When it comes to suffering, many people quote Romans 8:28 to say that every event that befalls us, no matter how horrible it may be, is always for our good. Do you believe God had Adam and Eve's best interests in mind when he pronounced the curses he did in the garden of Eden?"

WHY DOES GOD ALLOW SUFFERING?

The preacher quickly responded, "Yes, I do. Because with the curses, God also pronounced a plan of salvation when he said the woman's seed would crush the serpent's head. In this way, Adam and Eve would share eternity with God."

I thanked him. As I was walking away, mulling his answer over in my mind, I began thinking, *He didn't really answer the question. Even if there is a happy ending after a curse, wouldn't it have been better if he didn't have to curse us in the first place? Wouldn't it have been better if evil didn't exist?* Adam and Eve probably had a happy ending, even though the Bible never tells us clearly that they went to heaven. But did the human race really have to go through all that suffering so that *some* could make it to heaven? (See Matt. 7:13–14; John 14:6.) What about the billions of people who will die without accepting Christ's offer of salvation? Wouldn't God, if he really had *our* best interests in mind, create a world without the possibility of evil, where suffering wouldn't exist and everyone would go to heaven? How can we live in a world where suffering is so prevalent—sickness, wars, and death— and truly believe that God has *our* best interests in mind?

How could I ever convince an atheist—or myself—of that?

In *Is God Obsolete?* I started the book by raising the question: "Are we asking the proper questions, from the proper perspective, based on a proper understanding of the Almighty?" Sure, God could have created a world without the possibility of evil, where everyone would live a fairy-tale life on earth or in heaven. He could have even created the illusion in our minds that we had total free will. From our perspective, this sinless world without suffering would have been in *our* best interest, and it would have been the best world possible from *our* perspective.[8] But would it have been the best world possible from God's perspective? Would a world *without* the existence of evil and suffering have been in *God's* best interests?

In *Why Doesn't God Stop Evil?* we discussed in detail the good that comes out of evil from *God's perspective*. We also discovered that it is impossible for God to put *our* interests above *his* interests, because in doing so, God would be committing idolatry by placing greater worth in his creation than in himself. God tells us outright, "I make known the end from the beginning, from ancient times, what is still to come. I say: My purpose will stand, and I will do all that I please" (Isa. 46:10). "'To whom will you compare me? Or who is my equal?' says the Holy One" (Isa. 40:25).

Nowhere in the Bible do we read that God places our interests above his. Conversely, throughout the Bible God makes it quite clear that everything he does is for his glory—not our interests. Many believers quote the first part of Romans 8:28 without quoting the all-important last eight words: "who have been called according to his purpose."

God's singular *purpose* is to display his glory from his perspective. God cares deeply about us when we are suffering, but he cares even more deeply about his glory. As students of the Bible have pointed out, God's glory is primary—our good is secondary.

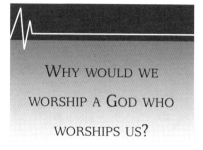

WHY WOULD WE WORSHIP A GOD WHO WORSHIPS US?

In today's evangelical climate, however, we have this backward. This is evident by the fact that most of our prayers involve asking God for more "stuff" or thanking God for what he has given us (the "good" that God brings our way). Very little of our prayers are devoted to actually praising God for *who he is.*

Furthermore, "according to his purpose" applies only to those believers whose primary goal is to live life completely for the glory of God—for "who he is" not "what's in it for me." You might be wondering: If conforming us through suffering into the likeness of his Son, Jesus Christ (see Rom. 8:29) is God's primary goal, why aren't more believers suffering? If God can direct a king's heart wherever he so desires (see Prov. 21:1), why can't God ignite a fire in millions more believers' hearts to get out there and radically serve him? If it's God's purpose—not humanity's—that always prevails (see Prov. 19:21), why has only a small fraction of the world's population throughout history been introduced to the gospel? And why has God allowed his church to slip into such a state of moral and doctrinal decay? Don't we worship an all-wise and all-powerful God? Obviously God has something more important in his agenda than the physical and spiritual good of the human race.

If you have trouble worshipping a God who would put his justice and glory above our good, consider this: All the great men and women of the Bible understood this fact—and it only served to further strengthen their trust, loyalty, worship, and wholehearted devotion to their Lord and Creator. In fact, I would argue that until you come to the understanding that God places his interests above ours, you cannot properly worship the God who exists.

Why would we worship a God who worships us?

You must understand this: Romans 8:28 is *not* advocating that all evil is for *our* good. Suffering, at its core, is not a one-way street that God is stuck on in his pursuit to attain some big prize in our lives. Suffering is not the last tool in God's toolbox that he uses in a last-ditch attempt to hammer us into the likeness of his Son. If it were, we'd see a whole lot more hammering going on in the church—and we'd see a whole lot more believers suffering like Job did.

But this isn't happening—at least not in the West. In other parts of the world, however, millions of Christians are suffering persecution for living a Christ-centered life—completely different from Christians in the West who usually suffer *less* overall for putting God first in their lives. Christians living moral lifestyles in the West usually suffer less physical and emotional pain than those living in immorality. As a medical doctor, I see the suffering that arises from alcohol abuse, illicit drugs, smoking, and promiscuous sex; permanent spinal cord injuries from drinking-and-driving accidents; severe head injuries from drunken bar-room fights; disability from smoker's lung disease; fatigue, weakness, and painful neuropathy from AIDS. God doesn't promise us health and wealth, but in his "law" of wisdom and sin, "A man reaps what he sows" (Gal. 6:7). This is one reason why many Christians aren't suffering more. But then again, Job was a very moral man, yet that didn't stop God from taking away almost everything he owned.

Why are most Christians today in the Western world not suffering like Job, if there are such great spiritual awards attached to our trials and tribulations? In God's providence, he has several tools at his disposal to mold us into the character of his dear Son. Suffering is certainly one of these tools, but it is not the only instrument in his toolbox.[9]

Some tout the cliché "Our life here on earth is a training for reigning"—meaning that the tribulations we suffer here on the planet are God's way of training us for reigning in the thousand years of Christ's reign on earth. But God wasn't *forced* to use the deaths of Ron and Arlene's boys to save souls, transform the family's faith, "train them for reigning," and bring them all closer to him. God didn't *need* to have Becki's leg amputated to bring about a revival in the local church. God doesn't *need* to use the tool of adversity at all in his everyday providential workings. He has many other options—many other "tools"—at his disposal.

As in Solomon's case, God is able to directly channel true spiritual understanding and wisdom to a believer's heart quicker than you can ask for it; he is able to richly develop our characters, grant us an understanding of his person, and instantaneously instill within us a deep passion for serving him—all without using adversity. Many godly heroes have suffered very little in their lifetimes. Again, look at how godly and upright Job was *before* he went through the suffering he did. That was likely the first time he experienced any significant degree of suffering in his life.[10]

If you still insist that God's *only reason* for allowing us to suffer is to produce some immediate good in the circumstances, you have a big, big problem on your hands. Because then you are left to ponder these inescapable questions the rest of your life: God, did you really have to take the life of my loved one to save this soul? Did you really have to strike me down with this unbearable illness to strengthen my faith? Did you really have to allow this person to rape me to bring about this good? If you really are all-wise and all-powerful, couldn't you have brought about this good by some other means?

If you believe that the *only reason* God allows us to suffer is to work some immediate good out of the adversity, then your life will remain an endless cycle of unanswerable questions.[11] Dr. Kuhlman tried to understand the good that came about from the death of his sixteen-year-old son, Keith.

> At the human level of understanding, I have trouble achieving the reconciliation of the death of my son and God's working for good. It defies logic. No rational judgment seems to support it.[12]

Often we can't see anything positive come out of our unutterable sorrow. Trying to rationalize our suffering by looking near at hand for some good can often bring about even more confusion and discouragement.

Romans 8:28 *must* be interpreted in the context of the entire Scriptures. God, the potter, did not create the clay for the clay's enjoyment and good—but for the potter's good and delight. If you want to interpret this verse more broadly—to say that absolutely everything that happens is for *our good*—it still cascades back to the King of kings. For our chief purpose here on earth, as God's elect, is to glorify God. And since suffering as a whole brings God more glory in the end (as we'll see later), then all suffering is for our good because we are bringing more glory to God through it all.

The ultimate reason Job suffered was not for *his* good; it was not to get back double the possessions he had in the beginning; it was not solely to strengthen his faith and give him a greater vision; it was not ultimately meant to help other hurting believers who would later read his story; it wasn't intended to prove the Devil wrong. The ultimate reason Job suffered was not in the small picture, but in the big picture—to bring, in the end, more glory to his Creator and Lord.

To see the big picture more clearly, the root reason for suffering, we must travel back for a last time to the very beginning.

IF YOU BELIEVE THAT
THE *ONLY REASON* GOD
ALLOWS US TO SUFFER
IS TO WORK SOME
IMMEDIATE GOOD OUT
OF THE ADVERSITY,
THEN YOUR LIFE WILL
REMAIN AN ENDLESS
CYCLE OF UNANSWERABLE
QUESTIONS.

Is God speaking to us through our suffering? It is dangerous and perhaps even unscriptural to torture ourselves by looking for his message in a specific throb of pain, a specific instance of suffering. The message may simply be that we live in a world with fixed laws, like everyone else. But from the larger view, from the view of all history, yes, God speaks to us through suffering—or perhaps in spite of suffering. The symphony he is composing includes minor chords, dissonance, and tiresome fugal passages. But those of us who follow his conducting through early movement will, with renewed strength, someday burst into song.[1]

—PHILIP YANCEY

6
THE ULTIMATE REASON
WE SUFFER

Nestled within Yancey's insightful quote is a sentence that some might quickly read without much thought: "The message may simply be that we live in a world with fixed laws, like everyone else." Could this one sentence hold part of the secret for why we suffer? Could this one road sign point us to the dazzling "sunset" in God's big picture of life?

Before we examine this road sign in more detail, read again carefully the quote by George MacDonald:

> Sometimes a thunderbolt will shoot from a clear sky; and sometimes, into the midst of a peaceful family—without warning of gathered storm above or slightest tremble of earthquake beneath—will fall a terrible fact, and from that moment everything is changed. The air is thick with cloud, and cannot weep itself clear. There may come a gorgeous sunset, though.[2]

WHY DOES GOD ALLOW SUFFERING?

Perhaps you've already had an inquisitive youngster ask you, "Why is the sky blue and a sunset red?" If you haven't, you probably will. When they do, just be thankful they didn't ask you where babies come from!

The answer to this frequently asked question lies in how light scatters after striking different molecules in the atmosphere. Space appears black to astronauts because few molecules exist to scatter the sun's rays. In contrast, when the sun is directly overhead, the rays hit the dust, vapor, and other particles in the air, causing the short wavelengths in the color spectrum (blue) to scatter much more than the longer wavelengths (red and orange). That's why the sky appears blue from our perspective here on earth.

But when the sun is on the horizon, it is farther away and must travel through a thicker layer of particles. The blue wavelengths of light are scattered so much they barely reach our eyes. In contrast, the longer wavelengths of color, such as red, orange, and pink break through the debris in the air to hit our eyes directly. That's why, for the most part, a sunset is red.

Two facets of God's sunset make up the big picture of life. George MacDonald talks about the thunderbolts, storms, and earthquakes in our sieges of suffering: "The air is thick with cloud, and cannot weep itself clear." But then he writes, "There may come a gorgeous sunset, though." You see, the thicker the air, often the more gorgeous the sunset. That's why some of the most spectacular sunsets are seen following huge wildfires or major volcanic eruptions, when tons of debris and chemicals are spilled into the atmosphere.

The same holds true in the spiritual realm. In our suffering here on earth, often the bigger the storm, or the greater the tragedy that erupts, the more beautiful the sunset of renewed hope and faith in God. Ron and Arlene would readily attest to this truth.

The second key feature of a sunset is the directness of the sun's rays. The brilliant colorations of a sunset and sunrise are visible only because we can see the longer wavelengths of the color spectrum. The shorter wavelengths essentially get filtered out.

We can also apply this analogy to our journey into understanding the Divine. If we want to see the most gorgeous sunset inside God's big picture, we have to be willing to look directly at the sun. If we ever hope to spy the most spectacular colors in God's sunset we must first filter out all the humanistic philosophy from our human spectrum and focus squarely on God's truth. If we don't, we will miss out on the most beautiful display of God's colors imaginable.

Let's say we look directly into the beautiful horizon of God's Word to see the most stunning sunset ever....

LOOKING UP

Evil men do not understand justice, but those who seek the
LORD understand it fully. (Prov. 28:5)

This one verse explains a lot, doesn't it? Try to explain to an unbeliever from God's Word why we suffer, and he or she will probably look at you as though you've been smoking something on a different planet. Nothing about suffering makes any sense to such a person. Why? Because he or she has very little or no initiative to seek the Lord. The unbeliever really doesn't want an answer unless it leaves him or her as the center of the universe.

If you're not ready, my friend, to submit your life to Christ—if you're not ready to seek the Lord—this chapter will make very little sense to you. You might as well close this book right now and go clean out your refrigerator. (I'm not kidding!)

In contrast to the unbeliever, Solomon says that the man or woman who seeks God will understand justice. If you are ready to seek God with all your heart—get ready!—you *will* understand justice, and you *will* see the striking "sunset," I promise you. *It is crucial that you and I grasp and take to heart the upcoming truths from God's trustworthy map.*

Most of us understand the basics of our penal system. Rob a bank, go to jail. Commit first-degree murder, get the death penalty or a life sentence. Park in a prohibited zone, and the tow-truck driver will find you—somehow. Wrongful actions naturally breed consequences in an ordered civilization. An intrinsic element of justice exists, whereby an individual is fairly rewarded for his or her moral actions.

God's justice works similarly. His ultimate justice in restoring divine order in the universe is achieved when an unrepentant sinner enters the lake of fire and a repentant believer enters heaven (on the basis of faith in Christ's atoning blood). But a *second* valuable component of justice we often overlook is *deterrence*. The public display of justice deters others from committing similar acts of evil. We experience less murder, theft, rape, and extortion in our world because of the threat of jail, flogging, fines, or the firing squad.

With this in the forefront of our minds, let's journey back to the garden of Eden where God pronounced certain curses on the world. God clearly gives us the answer in the first three chapters of Genesis for why suffering exists. The problem is that most people (believers included) don't like the answer.

For Our Good?

The prevailing mind-set in Christendom today embraces a God who allows suffering because it somehow has some benefit for believers. But what if there really are occasions when no personal good comes out of our suffering? Could you handle this? Could you continue to worship such a God who might allow you to suffer for no other reason than the sake of justice? God's passion for justice is the primary explanation for what we read in Isaiah 53:10. The Lord's will was to send his own Son to the cross to suffer and die. God chose justice over the physical well-being of his own dear Son. Could it be, then, that God values justice more than he does our temporal happiness and comfort?

W. E. Vine maintains, "God alone truly 'curses.' It is a revelation of His justice, in support of His claim to absolute obedience."[3] When Adam and Eve sinned, God cursed the pair, Satan, the ground, and every succeeding generation. Satan would one day suffer the final execution of his sentence in the lake of fire because of what Eve's offspring, Jesus Christ, accomplished at Calvary (see Gen. 3:14–15).

God cursed humanity by allowing for extreme bodily pain—particularly in childbearing (see v. 16). The curse of physical and spiritual death also fell upon the human race that day: "For dust you are and to dust you will return" (v. 19). A deteriorating creation, including thorns and thistles, would also haunt mankind (see vv. 17–18). These curses fell as a revelation of God's justice.

Now, notice something very important here: God didn't say to Adam and Eve, "I will curse you with pain, weeds, wrinkles, sickness, and death *so that I can directly bring some good out of it for you.*" God didn't say, "Adam and Eve, you are both going to age, get sick, suffer pain, and lose your son Abel *for your good.*" Look up the word *curse* in a dictionary sometime. *A curse does not directly benefit the person it falls upon.*[4] What possible good is there for a woman suffering horribly in labor? And don't say so that she will appreciate her baby that much more.

Reflecting on our own justice systems, the lawbreaker receives very little—if any—good when justice is finally handed down. What good did Timothy McVeigh get out of his death sentence for bombing and killing all those people in Oklahoma? Now it is true, in a roundabout way, that we all benefit from God's justice because evil is subdued (see 1 Peter 4:1–2). In *Why Doesn't God Stop Evil?* we discussed some of the reasons that God might permit us to endure hardships and tragedy. The brokenness we experience all around us—murders, assaults, shattered homes, earthquakes, tornados, drought, famine, sickness, rape, and any form of death—works to dramatically diminish the amount of evil in our hearts, especially pride. Adversity and suffering are naturally humbling. Could you imagine how wicked this world would be if everyone lived forever in perfect health, untouched whatsoever by any form of adversity?

Like unbelievers, believers also struggle with pride and other heinous sins of the heart against God. The reason we have so much difficulty understanding God in the area of suffering is that we can't see just how much our sins pain God every hour of every day. Pride and lying are two of the most despicable and stomach-heaving sins against God (see Prov. 6:16–19). God's retaliatory curses in the garden of Eden not only played a major role in helping to restore justice and order in the face of our rebellious acts, but these curses also played a key role of *deterrence* in restraining the amount of evil in our hearts—particularly pride. When we suffer God's curses, we are instantly humbled. This is one major reason that God allows these curses to play out today—even against believers.

Many godly believers through history have suffered one of the most physically and emotionally devastating evils there is: *rape*. Fists have been shaken and the questions asked, "How can God stand back and allow someone to sexually abuse one of his little children? Is this something a loving father could do? How does this fit into God's justice? Isn't this injustice from God's perspective?"

IF WE WOULD QUESTION GOD'S JUSTICE IN THE CASE OF RAPE OR MURDER, THEN WHY SHOULDN'T WE ALSO QUESTION GOD'S JUSTICE IN WHAT HAPPENED TO HIS ONLY SON, JESUS CHRIST?

Let me ask you this question: Are aging and death *injustice* from God's perspective? No. We all suffer the evils of the aging process, but few would blame God and lash out at him for our wrinkles. What we consider to be injustice in our world—rape, theft, extortion, and murder—are just as natural in God's justice system as the aging process. All of these "evils" are the result of sin, falling under the curses God pronounced in the garden of Eden. Why should we as Christians expect to be immune from the evils of rape and murder when it was our sins that caused God to bring down his curses upon the earth in the first place?

Rape and murder seem awful and disgusting to us because these evils happen suddenly and often to the most helpless and innocent. But imagine for a moment that the aging process was speeded up to the point where ninety-five years could fly by in forty seconds. Picture

a tiny baby before you. In a few blinks of an eye, the baby has grown into a teenager. Fifteen seconds later, the individual is now almost forty, with wrinkles and fat deposits starting to show. More wrinkles quickly appear. The eyes seem to sink back into the skull. Hair, shimmering only seconds before, is now stringy and gray. The horrifying transformation of a giggling baby to an old, toothless, hunched-back, shrunken frame of a ninety-five-year-old with cataracts, age spots, wrinkles, and atrophied muscles has happened in less than thirty-five seconds. While your mouth is still open in shock, the person dies right in front of you and grotesquely decays in a matter of seconds. Imagine if this horrific series of events flashed before your very eyes. Where would you now rank the aging process with rape and murder on the all time "evil list"?

To our eternal God, ninety-five years are less than a minute. This ugly aging and death process happens "instantly" before God's eyes every second of every day. Yes, God hates rape and murder more than we can possibly imagine; and he sometimes does protect us from these atrocities. But to God, they are no more heinous than the aging process. From God's perspective, are aging and death *injustice* on the person suffering these curses? No. And neither are rape and murder. If we could see everything through God's eyes, we would see that such evils as sexual abuse, torture, and murder, along with the aging process and death, all fall under the curses he unleashed upon mankind in the garden of Eden. We live in a broken and sin-cursed world. Why should we be astonished and angry when we suffer these curses? We should not be any more surprised that our sons and daughters are raped and murdered than that we are all aging and will one day all die. We deserve instant death for our sins—anything less is God's abundant warehouse of grace, no matter what event might befall us.

If we would question God's justice in the case of rape or murder, then why shouldn't we also question God's justice in what happened to his only Son, Jesus Christ? Christ is the only totally innocent person who has suffered on earth. Soldiers flogged Christ's back until it resembled raw hamburger. Then they drove large spikes into his wrists and hoisted him up on a cross. Was this fair?

WHY DOES GOD ALLOW SUFFERING?

Actually, in God's big picture of things, it was fair. No matter how much suffering you experience in life, God considers it "fair." Remember Isaiah 53:10 (NASB): "But the LORD was pleased to crush Him …" to crush His only Son. Not only was there no "injustice" from God's point of view in Christ's gruesome death, but it actually *pleased* the Father to see his innocent Son suffer. In the big picture of life, justice had prevailed. And God loves justice just as much as he loves His own Son. Christ took upon himself the sins of the world, allowing God the Father to wipe clean our record of sins, adopt us as his own dear children, and take us to heaven. The silver-tinged "clouds" of God's justice provided the most exquisite backdrop for the striking rays of his enduring love and mercy—and all for his highest glory.

Therefore, God's curses—his righteous acts of justice—are not ultimately for our good—*but for his good and divine glory.* Do you understand this very important truth? Curses such as aging, sickness, and death are not for our good—*but God's.* Most people, including the majority of believers, don't understand this; they just can't see how important justice is to God. They also can't see the strong vein of wisdom running throughout the Almighty's arm of justice in helping to deter the amount of evil in our world by working back to reduce the heinous sin of pride in all our hearts. That's because most people think of God as some cuddly, mushy-gushy, stuffed bear in the sky who wouldn't hurt a flea on a tick on a poodle.

Justice was so important to our heavenly Father that, in his matchless wisdom, he sent his own dear Son to earth to suffer and die a grotesque death so that the penalty of our sins would be paid. If justice weren't important to God, God would have never cursed mankind, and Christ would have never had to suffer as he did and die for our sins. On the other hand, if God's justice were the *only* perfection in operation, we would be instantly killed by his wrath and sent on a one-way trip to hell. Solomon says, "Evil men do not understand justice, but those who seek the LORD understand it fully" (Prov. 28:5).

Are you beginning to understand God's justice a little better?

THE ULTIMATE REASON WE SUFFER

AM I NOT PARDONED FROM MY SIN?

You might respond, "When Christ died on the cross, did he not die for *all* the consequences of my sins? If not, how can we honestly sing the popular hymn, 'There is pow'r, pow'r/Wonder-working pow'r/in the precious blood of the Lamb'?"

Is there power or isn't there?

There definitely is. It is true that when Christ died, he paid the penalty for your sin and removed the consequences of sin *in the spiritual realm*. Those who have accepted Christ as their Savior are born-again children of God, no longer slaves to sin; their sins are completely forgiven them by the power of Christ's shed blood; and they have received the promise of eternal life. *But Christ's death did not instantly remove the consequences of sin in the physical realm for a believer.* Christ's blood has power all right—but his blood cells didn't strong-arm justice and toss it away. God's justice still exists.

You have to understand that when Adam and Eve sinned, their sin nature was passed down to us. And because we all exist under the curse of Adam's original sin, we all suffer the physical consequences of these curses. "For all have sinned and fall short of the glory of God" (Rom. 3:23). "When Adam sinned, sin entered the entire human race. Adam's sin brought death, so death spread to everyone, for everyone sinned" (Rom. 5:12 NLT). I don't see anywhere in this verse where it says, "So death spread to everyone *except believers.*" Aging and sickness are all part of this curse of death.

We, as born-again sons and daughters of the heavenly King, have been pardoned in the *spiritual* kingdom, but the penalty of our sins will continue to follow us in this *earthly* kingdom.[5] How do we know this is true? Well, the Scriptures teach this very principle. For example, in 1 Peter 4:6 (NASB) we read of believers who died, "that though they are judged in the flesh as men, they may live in the spirit according to *the will of* God." Even believers are "judged in the flesh as men," yet all judgment ends for the believer when he or she dies and runs into the arms of God. Every single person on earth who has lived, or will ever live, is aging under God's judgment, and will one day die (see

Rom. 8:22–25). Had Christ's shed blood saved us immediately from the physical penalty of sin, believers here on earth would never grow old and frail—and they would never see the grave.

Thinking back to David's life, you'll remember that God completely forgave Israel's greatest king of his sins of adultery and murder. And because of saving faith, David was granted eternal life. *But the visible consequences of his sin in the physical realm followed him the rest of his days.* As believers, we are immediately freed from the penalty of our sin in the spiritual domain; but because all of us have prostituted ourselves and committed heinous acts of spiritual adultery against God in our hearts, we must bear the human consequences of these sins here on earth: consequences such as sickness, pain, toil, and death. God's laws of justice still exist.

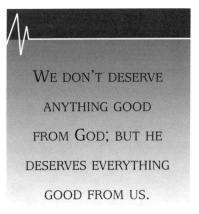

WE DON'T DESERVE ANYTHING GOOD FROM GOD; BUT HE DESERVES EVERYTHING GOOD FROM US.

God's justice is very wise—and very fair. I believe the "fixed laws" that Yancey speaks of are the laws God has ordained for the entire human race. In a perfect justice system, penalties will always result from breaking our government-made laws; likewise, in the Almighty's perfect justice system, penalties will always result from breaking his laws. And just as a prince or a president's daughter is not immune from the repercussions of unlawful actions, so we, as princes and princesses, sons and daughters of the King of kings, are not immune from the physical repercussions of our sinful actions here on earth. Perfect justice demands that a prince and a pauper who commit the same crime pay the same penalty. The perfectness of God's character demands that his laws of justice extend equally, fairly, and fully to every person on earth. God, as the altogether sovereign ruler of the universe, is allowed, however, to pardon whomever he pleases; yet he is not obligated in any way to protect the believer from the corporal wages of sin in this earthly kingdom (see Rom. 6:23).

THE ULTIMATE REASON WE SUFFER

When God finally spoke to Job out of the whirlwind, he asked the patriarch point blank, "Would you discredit my justice? Would you condemn me to justify yourself?" (Job 40:8). Notice that God didn't say, "Job, would you discredit my *love?* Would you discredit my *wisdom?* Would you discredit my *mercy?* Would you discredit my *power?* Would you discredit that I have your *best intentions* in mind?" No. God said, "Would you discredit my *justice?*" All suffering, no matter what it is, stems from God's justice.

The root reason we suffer here on earth, then, is not so that God can produce some good out of it from our perspective. It's not so that he can save more souls. It's not so that he can send us some message in our suffering to make us more spiritual. The ultimate, fundamental reason—the root cause—behind why God allows us to suffer is to satisfy his justice. But again, this is an answer that most people don't want to hear. They'd rather listen to preachers, televangelists, or New Age gurus spout off "touchy feely" stuff that makes listeners feel good than actually hear what God has to say on the matter in his Word.[6]

The primary reason God allowed my dear grandmother to die two weeks before the birth of her first great grandson was that she, like every other person on earth, had sinned. Consequently, her sickness and death were the result of God's laws of justice revealed in the curses he pronounced in the garden of Eden.

Similarly, the fundamental reason God allowed sixteen-year-old Becki to lose her leg was not so that he could bring about a church revival; neither did God plant a malignant cell in Becki's leg to punish her for a particular sin she or her father had committed; God allowed, by way of Becki's defective DNA, for the malignant cancer cells to form and replicate in her leg because it harmonized with the "fixed laws"—the curses—he pronounced upon mankind in the garden of Eden. Becki lost her leg, not ultimately for her good or the good of her church or the good of anyone else, but to fulfill the justice of God. Remember: *We don't deserve anything good from God; but he deserves everything good from us.*

In contrast to my grandmother's death, a clear, observable good came about because of the deaths of Ron and Arlene's three boys. But they didn't lose their three sons so that souls could be won for Christ. The root cause behind why Vaughn, Brent, and Curtis died was for God's good—to satisfy his justice. (The reason all of us will eventually die stems back to God's justice.) There might very well have been a genetic component to Vaughn and Brent's struggle with depression. God allowed their sickness to develop and escalate in this broken world to the point that the boys took their own lives. Had it been in God's sovereign will, he could have easily prevented their deaths, maybe by granting them more spiritual wisdom and understanding or healing them of any depression. But instead, he allowed his "fixed laws"—the curses he decreed in the garden of Eden—to operate largely unopposed.

Curtis ultimately didn't die in the snowmobile accident so that his family's faith would be strengthened. Curtis died because God allowed the law of sin to overlap with his "law of chance"—thereby satisfying his justice.[7] God wasn't punishing Ron, Arlene, and their boys for a specific sin; rather, God was allowing his justice to operate because of original sin and the curses he pronounced in the garden.

Romans 6:23 says, "For the wages of sin is death," physical *and* spiritual death. When your employer hands you your check at the end of the week, do you get angry with your boss? Do you feel guilty, thinking that your boss is punishing you for some specific error you made? No, because you *deserve* your wages. You worked hard for them. Why would you be angry or bitter at your employer for giving you what you rightfully deserve? He's not punishing you.

If you are having difficulty linking punishment with our "deserved wages," then consider the more classic illustration of a child who steals a chocolate bar from the local 7-Eleven. Normally we don't throw small children into prison or chop off their arms for stealing; but when they are caught, often the punishment involves the humbling act of returning the chocolate bar along with making an apology to the store owner.

However you wish to look at the crime–punishment connection between original sin and suffering, the punishment is always fair. Would you think it unfair for the child to be humbled by returning the chocolate bar with an apology? Actually, if anything is unfair it is that we're still allowed to live despite the fact that we commit heinous sins against God in our heart every day.

Likewise, when God pays us the deserved "wages" of our sins—sickness, aging, and death—we shouldn't become angry with God or feel that we are being punished for some specific wrongdoing. Why? Because God is just giving us what we deserve. In God's sight, we worked hard for these wages.

This is so vitally important for us to understand. This "salary" spoken of in Romans 6:23 is not God's way of "punishing us" for some particular sin we've committed. Rather, the "wages" the apostle Paul is speaking of in Romans is a fixed sum paid out by God to every person on earth in accordance with original sin and our sin natures as a whole. God is not "punishing us" in the way that many people think. Read Romans 5:12 (NLT) again carefully: "When Adam sinned, sin entered the entire human race. Adam's sin brought death, so death spread to everyone, for everyone sinned."

Now, what would happen if your employer decided to withhold your wages? Wouldn't you shout, "Unfair!" With God, however, when he *pays us our wages* we shout, "Unfair!" We shake our fists at our Creator and cry out, "God, I deserve to live out a long, pain-free, adversity-free life of pleasure!" Read through the Bible from cover to cover and you will see that we deserve no such thing. The only thing we deserve is death for the rebellious sins of pride, envy, greed, selfishness, and hate that we flaunt in God's face every day. If you want to criticize God's justice, the only fault you can find with your Creator is that he doesn't give you your deserved wages sooner—that being physical death. While we are living, however, any suffering we face is always less than we merit (see Ps. 103:10; Ezra 9:13). An unbeliever can't understand any of this. Neither can many believers.

When it comes to sickness, can God be faulted if he allows us to get some of our paychecks midweek, rather than at the end of the workweek? When God permits some of us to fall ill, maybe with diabetes, osteoarthritis, cancer, or heart disease, God is just allowing us part of our wages a little earlier than expected. But make no mistake, my friend, *every single person on this earth will eventually be paid.* We all exist under God's curses that he pronounced upon original sin (see Gal. 3:10; 6:7–8; James 1:15). We are all aging and will one day all die because of the adulterous acts of sin we have collectively committed against God. In God's magnificent justice and fairness, we all get the same wage; it's just that God allows some of us to have an advance on our paychecks sooner than others.

Just as you can't fault your employer for paying you early, you can't fault God for giving us our deserved wages a little sooner than anticipated. Some will receive their full paychecks at ten years of age. Some at eighteen. Some at forty. And some at ninety-three. Whatever age you may be when you leave this world, this you can be sure of: *We will one day all be paid in full when we die.*[8] Again, if God's justice were the only perfection in operation, all of us would have received our full paychecks by now; none of us would be alive.

Dr. MacArthur reminds us, "It's not your right to live. It's God's grace that gives you life."[9] God's grace allows us to take every single breath of our lives, only we don't deserve it. The world-renowned Bible teacher continues, "We live under constant mercy, so when justice shows up we're shocked. We get so used to grace that we don't understand justice."[10] Rabbi Harold Kushner wrote the well-known book *When Bad Things Happen to Good People*. MacArthur says that one day he's going to write a book titled *Bad Things Happen to Everybody.*[11]

Understanding that we do not deserve to be alive at this very moment really clears up a lot of confusion and questions about God's character. You see, it wasn't Job's right to live pain-free in a disease-free, disaster-free, and death-free world. Even though he was labeled an "upright man," it was only by the grace of God that Job was allowed to live at all. Every oxygen molecule Job breathed had been leased from God with no money down, no security deposit, and no payments for life. Moreover, it was only by the grace of God that Job was "upright" to begin with.

Similarly, it was only by the supreme grace of God that Becki, Vaughn, Brent, Curtis, Dr. Kulhman's son Keith, and my grandmother were allowed to live another second after they committed their first act of sin against their Creator. Actually, because of original sin, we don't deserve even to be born into this world. Dr. William McRae, president emeritus at Tyndale University College and Theological Seminary, correctly points this out: "Today we seem to have enshrined, as our fourth inalienable right, the right to be free from suffering, conflict, opposition and pain."[12] A close study of Scripture reveals that we hold no such right.

But praise God, he has chosen to pardon some from the spiritual and physical consequences of sin in eternity. Romans 6:23 has a happy ending: "For the wages of sin is death, *but the gift of God is eternal life in Christ Jesus our Lord.*" Even though we will all die, God has chosen to pardon those from spiritual death who accept Christ's atoning blood as full payment for their sins.

Here again is further evidence of God's mercy and grace that no amount of ink can possibly do justice to.

ONE BEAUTIFUL MOSAIC

I realize that if you are grieving the loss of someone very close to you at this moment, or enduring some other terrible adversity in your life, these candid truths may be unsettling and very difficult to understand. And as I warned you at the beginning of this book, they may cause you to become quite angry with me—and with God. In our modern, feel-good world we would rather not hear about sin and God's justice (which is why most preachers rarely speak on the subjects); but the truth is, they both exist. I would be deceiving you greatly if I tried to paint any different picture for why we suffer. And I could not live with my conscience, knowing that I had purposely misled you to believe something different—even if it meant selling hundreds of thousands of books. The truth is, we all live in a broken world where we all suffer the physical consequences of our sin nature. *We owe our Creator absolutely everything; he owes us absolutely nothing—except hell.*

As we discovered earlier, the most gorgeous sunsets are seen when there is smoke or other debris in the air. One of the most beautiful pictures I have ever seen was a sunset framed by striking mountains, trees, clouds, a darkened sky, and a big bolt of lightning. The rich red, orange, and yellow hues of the sunset were even more incredible because of the smoke in the air—possibly caused by a fire when lightning struck.

In a similar way, God's mosaic displays maximum beauty when "smoke" is in the air. God's beautiful mosaic of life includes blazing suns, trickling brooks, luscious vegetation, and towering trees—but also thunderbolts, smoke, and fire. And we might wonder why God would want such destructiveness in his prized mosaic.

Perhaps you have endured years of physical or emotional suffering, and your "life piece" in God's perfect mosaic might make up part of a thunderbolt. Maybe you are an unbeliever—ridiculing, testing, or maybe even murdering or raping God's children. Your life piece might form the fire or smoke in God's mosaic. As hard as it is for us to understand, the thunderbolts, smoke, and fire of cancer, death, wars, famine, earthquakes, and all manner of sin work together to help create the most gorgeous sunset from God's perspective. The overwhelming beauty and striking rays of God's matchless character— his justice, wrath, love, mercy, grace, and wisdom—could *never* be displayed on this earth to its fullest potential of beauty without the thunderbolts, smoke, and fire of life (see Ps. 76:10; Rom. 9:22; cf. 9:18, 23; 11:32).

Consider this as well: Without your life, God's mosaic is incomplete. It doesn't matter if you are a self-sacrificing saint who feeds homeless children or an atheist dictator guilty of years of genocide, you are very important to God. And no matter where God fits your life piece into his exquisite mosaic, it will fit perfectly into a tapestry of millions of other pieces to form the loveliest mosaic to bring God the highest degree of glory possible.

Often, though, we don't really care all that much about God's prized artwork—his glory. Usually we want only one "ingredient" of God—such as his love or his mercy—rather than accepting the whole of his perfectly balanced being. Many children will eat spoonfuls of sugar straight out of the sugar bowl if allowed. Often we act like the youngest generation, wanting to taste and experience only the "sugar" of who God is.

We are multidimensional individuals. So why do we continually try to mold God into a one-dimensional being within our minds? Why do we invent a God we can live with, and then do everything possible to try to make our experiences fit this created being? Millions of people are asking some pretty tough "God questions" on suffering, but many don't want to hear the answers unless they leave them in the center of their universe eating out of a giant bowl of sugar. Even many believers don't want to hear the answers unless they fit with the pre-conceived image of the god they've formed in their minds. And for many believers, this preconceived image embraces a God who would not allow us to suffer unless there is some good in it *for us*. If we ever hope to understand God on this tough subject, we must break out of the prevailing mind-set held by most Christians that suffering is only for *our* immediate or future good.

A respected author once wrote that if God doesn't answer our prayers for a miraculous physical healing, it is "only because He has some better thing in store for us which time or eternity will reveal."[13] This author is correct when he says that time and eternity will more clearly reveal to us the mosaic displaying the ultimate reason we suffer. God definitely has a good reason for why he allows us to go through the trials we do. But even when God uses suffering to achieve a secondary goal, to refine us into more mature and steadfast believers, it is still ultimately for *his good*—not ours.

God says to his child Israel:

> See, I have refined you, though not as silver; I have tested you in the furnace of affliction. *For my own sake, for my own sake, I do this.* How can I let myself be defamed? I will not yield my glory to another. (Isa. 48:10–11)

"FOR MY OWN SAKE, FOR MY OWN SAKE, I DO THIS"

So you see, dear friends, this mosaic is for God's glory—not ours. Life is not about us; it's about God. Likewise, suffering is not about us; it's about God.

WHY DOES GOD ALLOW SUFFERING?

At times God allows us to endure extreme amounts of suffering for the *only* reason that his justice will prevail. This statement is not meant to discourage you in life, but to help you better understand God's character—particularly his justice. Take a look at the believers who become cold toward God in the face of suffering, or those who become atheists or agnostics because someone close to them died. Could God not have foreseen the terrible consequences of this suffering? If so, why did he allow it? God pronounced the curses he did in the garden of Eden because he loves justice just as much as he loves you and me. Actually, he loves himself more than he loves you and me. If he didn't, he would be committing idolatry.

Many people still bang their heads against these truths and shout, "Unfair!" at God. Is God really being unfair, however? We love to see justice, don't we? We love it when a criminal like Charles Manson or Timothy McVeigh is placed behind bars. Why then is it so difficult to believe that God, our Creator, who created us in his image, also loves justice? Why can't we just let God be God and accept that his marvelous perfections including his love, mercy, wrath, righteousness, *and justice* are all perfectly balanced in his flawless character?

The answer for why we suffer is found in the first three chapters of Genesis. But again, it is the answer few people want to hear. When someone is grieving terribly, we try to comfort them by saying, "Just wait. God will bring some good out of all this suffering for you." But is this statement biblically correct? If we ever hope to understand God on the difficult subject of suffering, we have to closely examine God's Word as mature believers and wholeheartedly accept the answers that God gives us. Believing a lie, or telling people a lie, will not help at all on our journey to intimacy with the Divine.

When we suffer, justice is served, evil is restrained, and God's sovereignty, holiness, and moral law are upheld and kept in balance with his love, mercy, and grace. And in the end, more glory is duly brought to God's righteous and hallowed name. Some good may come out of our suffering from our perspective: Souls may be won for Christ; relatives and friends may re-dedicate their lives to God; our faith may become stronger. But from God's perspective, that is not the ultimate reason he allowed us to go through the deep waters of affliction. The ultimate reason we suffer is the same reason we were created—for the glory of God. This is the big picture—the most beautiful mosaic— behind why Job, and everyone else in the world, suffers.

Never forget: God's good reason for allowing us to suffer—the root cause of all our trials and tribulations—is not seen in the small picture of everyday life events, or in the individual "life pieces" in the Master's hands, or in some good that will befall us at some point in the future; but rather, the root cause of our suffering is contained in the brushstrokes of God's justice as seen in his big picture—the incomparable "mosaic"—of God's overall plan for the universe.

God's silence is in no way indicative
of His activity or involvement in our lives.
He may be silent, but He is not still.[1]

—Dr. Charles Stanley

7

SEEING THE COMPLETE SUNSET

Perhaps the portrait I've painted in your mind so far is one you've never seen before. Maybe the lines I've sketched for you seem a little harsh. The colors and tone may still feel somewhat cold and detached. The texture might feel bumpy and inconsistent. Perhaps the objects still appear somewhat disordered—out of place inside such a noble picture frame of infinite worth. The portrait of God I've painted so far may appear less than lovely in your mind; if so, chances are it's because this picture is only half finished.

I trust that this final illustration will add the needed finishing touches to this unique portrait—and to the book as a whole.

THE GREATEST PARDON EVER

The story unfolds of a father and his two sons—ages thirty-three and twenty-five—living in the small northern hemisphere country we'll call Cosmosia.[2]

WHY DOES GOD ALLOW SUFFERING?

The father, as the most respected citizen in the prosperous country, is the only chief justice in Cosmosia's supreme court. Every case that is brought up from a lower court comes before him, and him only. His decision, no matter what it may be, is final and binding. The father, who delights greatly in justice, is also Cosmosia's sole lawmaker. Not only does the father enforce the laws but he also makes them.

One day, while the judge is presiding at his bench, a young, good-looking man dressed in expensive designer clothes is brought before him. The lower court had convicted him of second-degree murder—a crime punishable by capital punishment, according to Cosmosia's criminal law. As part of Cosmosia's civil law, the murderer must also automatically pay restitution to the victim's family in the amount of $150,000. The district and defense attorneys are both present to argue their cases in this critical court trial.

"How do you plead?" the judge asks.

"I plead not the least guilty, Your Honor!" blurts out the young man—a smirk across his face. His lack of remorse is obvious.

After hearing the case at length, the judge calls the accused before him. "Young man, I have heard all the evidence laid out against you. And I uphold the lower court's decision. I find you guilty of second-degree murder. Your assets will be sold and $150,000 will be given to the victim's family. Then you will be sentenced to death by lethal injection." Cursing and swearing, the young man is marched away.

The next day, another young man is brought before the judge. This time, though, in striking difference to the previous criminal, the accused is a straggly, harelipped, elfin man in his mid twenties. As the only supreme court justice in Cosmosia, the father is the only person who has the authority to rule over the case. But there is a personal, heart-wrenching facet to it all, for this young man is the judge's youngest son. Adopted from an orphanage as a toddler, he now stands before his father for the crime of murder. In a fit of rage one day, the twenty-five-year-old had taken a knife and stabbed to death his older brother—*the father's only son by birth.*

As he is being led into the courtroom, the son sees his father. Breaking away from the guard, the son hobbles forward, collapsing to the courtroom floor just a few feet from his father's bench. Tears streaming down his cheeks, he sobs uncontrollably, "Father, I'm sorry! I am so sorry.... I didn't mean to kill him. I beg you, please forgive me. I would do anything—anything!—to undo what I've done. But please, Father, have mercy on me. Have mercy on me, I pray."

The father, overcome with grief, drops his head into his hands, weeping loudly. Everyone in the courtroom knows how much the father loved his two sons. No one in Cosmosia had ever experienced the terrible pain this father was suffering. He had just buried his only birth son, and now his youngest son, for whom he would do absolutely anything, is sobbing on the floor before him, begging for his forgiveness. The father's heart lies broken in a thousand pieces.

A few minutes pass before the father slowly raises his head. Wiping away the tears, he speaks in a calm and tender voice, "Son, I am very, very angry at your actions. You have caused me a tremendous amount of heartache and pain." He pauses for a few seconds. "But I forgive you. I truly do."

Collecting himself, the father straightens up in his chair. "Still, I must ask you: How do you plead?"

"I am guilty, Father," is the son's only response.

The hard-line district attorney steps forward. "Your Honor. The accused has admitted before the court that he is guilty. By the laws of Cosmosia, the penalty for second-degree murder is death. Yesterday you sentenced a young man to lethal injection for the same crime. Today, justice must triumph by handing out the same sentence."

At this point, the son's defense attorney steps forward. "Your Honor. I agree that my client is guilty by his own admission. And by the laws of this land he does deserve death by lethal injection. But Your Honor, you drafted a clause in the laws that allows you the executive right to pardon whomever you choose. Your Honor, please have mercy on your beloved son and pardon his crime."

"But, Your Honor," blurts out the district attorney, "you love justice and must treat everyone fairly. This man deserves death!"

The courtroom drips silence. The father, crushed in his spirit, gazes down at his son. Their eyes lock for what seems like an eternity....

Finally, the father softly speaks, "My dear son. I love you more than you will ever realize. More than a hundred parents passed you over in the orphanage before you were four years of age. You were not the best-behaved child. You were not the cutest child. Nor were you the most gifted. But I loved you with all my heart. And I chose you that day to be my son when no one else wanted you."

The tears begin to well up again in the father's eyes. "I love you, my son. But as judge of Cosmosia I also love justice. You are guilty of murder. You have sinned, not only against your brother, but also against me. By the laws I have enacted, you deserve death."

The district attorney's eyes are already celebrating.

"There's something I never told you, Son."

The son appears surprised, "What is it, Father?"

The father struggles to continue. "When you were five you developed severe liver disease and the doctors said you would die without a liver transplant. There were no organs available."

"Father, the doctors told me it came from a guy who was killed in a car crash—"

"No, Son."

"Then, who gave me the—?"

"Your thirteen-year-old-brother. He voluntarily donated half of his liver."

The son stands stunned. "My ... my brother? *He* was the one?"

"Yes. But when you stabbed him, the knife penetrated his liver. The surgeons couldn't repair it in time." Tears well up in the father's eyes. "They said he probably would have survived if he hadn't gone through with the transplant operation when he was younger. He was totally innocent. He gave his life to save yours ... and you killed him."

The son breaks down, weeping uncontrollably. His loud sobbing can be heard well beyond the courtroom doors. "I deserve to die. Oh please, Father. I cannot bear to live with my conscience!"

The defense attorney turns back to the judge. "Your Honor, what is your verdict?"

The father stares at his son with sad, pain-filled eyes. His son has brought him unimaginable grief and suffering. Straightening up in his chair, he looks down at his papers then back up. "As the chief justice—the only justice—of Cosmosia's supreme court, I have the executive right to pardon whomever I will. Just as it would not tarnish my justice in the least to sentence you to death, neither would it tarnish my justice in the least to pardon you."

There is another lengthy pause.

"By my sovereign power and authority, I hereby pardon you from the sentence of death. And I hereby declare you not guilty. Any record of wrongdoing will be completely erased from your criminal record."

"But, Your Honor—" shouts the district attorney.

"Silence!" retorts the father. "I and I alone have the power to pardon and sentence whomever I choose! Besides … it was my own son who was murdered." Turning back to his youngest son, he continues. "Your guilt has been wiped away."

The son can't believe his ears. "You—you aren't mad at me?"

"No, my dear son. You hurt me deeply, but I have forgiven you."

"Thank you! Thank you so much, Father!" the son exclaims. "I am a changed person! I really am. I will do my very best to make you proud of me!"

The father remains quiet, though. Looking back up, he speaks once more, "Son, your criminal record has been wiped clean. But your actions have spawned consequences. To make things right, I am ordering you to pay $150,000 to the victim's family—namely myself and your brother's wife."

"But, Father, I don't have $150,000."

"Then, Son, according to my civil laws, those who cannot pay must be ordered to work in a strict labor camp until restitution is made."

The district attorney stands in silence with a sneer on his face. He knows the deplorable living conditions that exist at these work camps and the suffering the son will endure. Yet the father knows even better. As a teenager, the father was falsely accused of stealing an expensive sports car and sentenced to suffer a brutal work term of two years. He finished his time before the truth was eventually exposed that he was completely innocent. The father knows better than anyone else what his son is about to go through.

WHY DOES GOD ALLOW SUFFERING?

The locked stone rooms in these rugged camps resemble jail cells more than regular living quarters. Because of Cosmosia's northern latitude, the rooms are often bitterly cold in the winter months. The grueling work conditions require workers to toil many hours a day in an open rock quarry. The cold, the exhaustion, the food scraps, the blisters, the painful joints, and the sickness in these camps are horrible. Some have even died from major illnesses. But these camps have served their purpose well. Not only is justice brought about in the form of monetary restitution for victims' families, but also criminal activity in the country is deterred overall.

Having survived such a camp himself, the father knows that his son's imposed work term will help the young man to become a better person. Throughout much of his life, his son has struggled with pride, anger, and selfishness. His preceding rebellion has greatly strained the relationship with his father. The father knows his son will leave the camp a changed person; yet this is not the primary reason he sentenced his son to the grueling toil. The underlying reason his son will suffer in the camp is that of justice—the consequences of his unlawful actions.

On his first workday, the son finds himself in the middle of an exposed rock quarry, swinging a heavy pickax. Already his hands are blistered and bleeding. The cold, damp wind bites at his face and penetrates his clothes. Exhausted, hungry, flustered, numb, and sore, he can't endure another minute. His knees suddenly buckle and he falls backward toward the uneven rock—but two strong arms catch him just before he hits the ground. Opening his eyes, the son finds himself in his father's arms. "It's okay, Son. I'm here."

Picking up his son, the father gently carries him back to his room. On the hard cot, the father hugs his son close to his chest. The son, weeping, with barely enough strength to speak, whispers, "It really hurts, Father."

"I know, Son. I know...." And the father hugs his son even closer.

Day after day, the father remains by his son's side. Encouraging him to go on. Nourishing him with home-cooked food he has brought in. Strengthening him when all strength is gone. And best of all, comforting him by his presence alone—holding his crying son into the wee hours of the night. Often the father hugs his trembling son tight to his chest in the still darkness. The son can't see his father during these darkest moments, but he can feel his father's arms wrapped tight around him. And the son knows that with his father's help, he will get through these tough times.

His father's tears and love are the only assurance he needs.

ADOPTED, PARDONED, AND ALWAYS GOD'S CHILD

> This is what the LORD says: "Let not the wise man boast of his wisdom or the strong man boast of his strength or the rich man boast of his riches, but let him who boasts boast about this: that he understands and knows me, that I am the LORD, who exercises kindness, justice and righteousness on earth, for in these I delight," declares the LORD. (Jer. 9:23–24)

Though the above illustration is not perfect (few illustrations are), it does paint a beautiful portrait of God's rich character. This illustration helps us to better understand the different roles God plays as our sovereign ruler, advocate, judge, friend, comforter, savior, and loving heavenly Father. It helps us to better understand how God can delight in kindness, justice and righteousness all at the same time.

God, as our creator and ruler, holds the exclusive right to be worshipped. He also holds the unrestricted privilege to impose upon those who break his laws any penalty he deems fair in his justice. And because all of us have sinned, breaking God's heart and his laws, we are all guilty before the supreme ruler of the universe. Romans 3:23 says, "For all have sinned and fall short of the glory of God." "All have sinned" is in the past tense, but "fall short" is in the present tense. We have all missed the mark, failed God, committed wicked acts of spiritual adultery against God in the past, and we *continue* to sin, to "fall short," come behind, the glory of God—what God expects from us. Therefore, God's justice is seen on every single member of the human race right now because "*all* have sinned" and continue to sin against him. That's why God's justice, including sickness, aging, and death, plays no favorites in our world.

Christ, however, as our advocate (our "defense attorney") pleads our case before God in the Almighty's courtroom. Our sins nailed Christ, the only begotten Son of God, to the cross when he was only thirty-three. In a sense, we were the ones who murdered God's Son, even though he voluntarily gave his life for us (just like the older son who voluntarily went through the liver transplant operation to save his younger brother, yet in the end it cost him his life). But Christ, our Savior, the same person we helped murder, now stands beside us as our trusted friend and mediator. He says to his Father, "Yes, this son or daughter of yours is guilty and deserves death." Christ, though, holds up his wrists marred with the nail imprints: "But by my shed blood, a clause in your law allows you to pardon whomever you choose—even those who nailed me to the cross."

The Devil (the "district attorney" and great accuser) stands in the same courtroom, proclaiming our guilt. "Look what they did to your Son!" But God, who chose us as misfits out of the orphanage when we least deserved it, has adopted us into his family and completely pardoned us from the penalty of eternal death (see John 1:12; 14:18; Eph. 1:4–6).

The Righteous One, as our Lord and judge, has totally forgiven us of our sins if we have accepted by faith his Son's death on the cross as full payment for our sin debt. Our "criminal record" is wiped clean. In God's eyes, we as true believers are totally innocent because of Christ's work on the cross. However, our everyday sins of pride, selfishness, greed, and deceit still break God's laws. And God's justice is required to restore order to the universe. We have greatly pained God and broken his heart more than we will ever realize. Though we as believers are deemed not guilty in the spiritual realm ("criminal law"), the consequences will not go away in the physical realm ("civil law"). And it is these consequences that bring about suffering in our earthly "work camps." To think of a modern illustration that to some extent parallels this truth, consider that O. J. Simpson was pronounced not guilty of murder in criminal court, but he was found guilty in civil court and ordered to pay millions of dollars. Nevertheless, O. J. walked away from the trials with no criminal record.

As the all-wise judge, God uses suffering to satisfy his justice—to make things right in his eyes. God allows these consequences of the original sin to transform our faith and draw us closer to him—just as it did for the son in the story above. Yet the underlying reason we suffer is not to enhance our relationship with God, or to save souls who are looking on, but rather to satisfy the corrective justice of God. And because all suffering is very humbling, evil is greatly restrained.

But we are still blinded by God's love. Believers and unbelievers alike frequently raise the question, "How can a good God of love allow so much suffering in our world?" The root reason behind why we suffer has absolutely nothing to do with God's love, but it has everything to do with God's justice. The more appropriate question we should be asking is, "How can a good God of justice allow us to live?"

I would encourage you to read back over the story above, putting yourself in the younger son's shoes. Think back on all the times you have broken God's laws *and* his heart. Did you deserve to be chosen and adopted into God's loving family when God knew you would murder his Son? Do you realize the horrendous price Christ had to pay on the cross to pardon you from your sins and wipe your record clean? Do you now see why it is that we as believers are pronounced not guilty by our judge, yet we still suffer in life? Is all of this starting to make more sense?

I pray that it is. And I pray that when you are hurting, you will remember that God is always right beside you, counting all your tears. David says to God, "You have collected all my tears in your bottle. You have recorded each one in your book" (Ps. 56:8b NLT). Our heavenly Father knows *exactly* the number of tears you cry. He is with you every waking moment of every day, actively comforting, strengthening, and helping you, no matter what adversity you may be facing in this earthly work camp we live in.

"[God] may be silent," says Dr. Charles Stanley, "*but He is not still.*"[3]

WHY DOES GOD ALLOW SUFFERING?

WHY GOD DOESN'T PERFORM MORE MIRACLES

Perhaps you're thinking that everything about God's justice and these "fixed laws" seems so cut and dry. If all of mankind is sentenced to suffer the consequences for breaking God's laws, is there any point in praying for healing—or praying for a release from any type of adversity? Aren't we asking for something we don't deserve?

The answer is, yes, we are praying for something we don't deserve. But that doesn't mean we shouldn't pray. A true miracle of healing requires that God pardon us in his justice from his "civil law." Another of my books explains how God does instantly and fully pardon some from such sicknesses as cancer, heart disease, and genetic defects, although such miracles are very uncommon. This book explains why they are uncommon—because pardons, by definition, are rare; not only in our earthly courts, but also in God's *heavenly court*.[4] When we pray for a miracle of healing, what we are actually doing is coming before God in his courtroom and throwing ourselves on his mercy, petitioning him to release us, or someone we care about deeply, from the physical consequences of this broken and sin-cursed world. The next time you pray for a miracle of healing for yourself or your loved one, I would encourage you to do so, all the while being mindful of exactly what you are asking for. An attitude that *demands* that God pardon us from his curses of aging, sickness, and death is presumptuous to say the least.

Growing up in a world where we loudly proclaim God's love, yet quietly demote his justice, this "courtroom" line of thinking feels alien to us. We think that a prayer is a prayer is a prayer, asking God for basically the same thing—his time, assistance, and kindness. Often we think that asking God to miraculously heal us is like asking the chief justice of the supreme court to donate blood for thirty minutes. It doesn't seem like much effort to save a life, right?

Friends, God doesn't look at our prayers for healing in this light. He doesn't say, "Well, I guess I could spare some time and power to heal Bill of his prostate cancer or Nancy of her heart disease." God views our prayers for miraculous physical healing somewhat like a supreme court judge would view a request from a mother asking that her son receive a rare pardon based strictly on compassionate grounds.

God may not grant us a complete pardon in our sickness, but he often does lessen our sentence. As a specialist who treats patients with musculoskeletal pain, I have a complete armamentarium of pain medications, topical ointments, steroid injections, therapeutic modalities, and rehabilitation strategies to help patients deal with their nagging pain. Never before in the history of medicine have there been so many methods available to help ease our suffering. Even the dentist nowadays has topical freezing ointments to hold on the inside of our mouths so that we feel little or nothing of the needle while the anesthetic is being injected. Imagine what our relatives had to endure with a toothache more than a century ago! The thought struck me one day, *Am I somehow thwarting God's justice by helping to relieve part or all of my patients' suffering when this was part of God's curse that fell in the garden of Eden?*

I quickly reached the conclusion that no, I wasn't thwarting God's justice, but rather acting as a messenger of his mercy. Perhaps one of the most unrecognized and least valued of God's perfections in the past half century has been his mercy in the way of medical advances. We take so much for granted, yet only a very small percentage of all the world's population since the beginning of time has been the recipient of such extravagant kindness and mercy from the Almighty. We expect so much from our hospitals and doctors, yet we fail to realize that it is only because of God's mercy that most of us endure so little physical suffering in our lifetimes.

Unrecognized by us, then, most of our prayers for physical healing draw on God's unparalleled mercy—not his managerial assistance. Failing to understand this leads to all manner of confusion and discouragement. Dr. Conway, at the height of his frustration and anger, said, "I think [God] was so busy finding a parking spot for a little old lady that He didn't have time to save Becki's leg."[5]

WHY DOES GOD ALLOW SUFFERING?

WHERE IS GOD WHEN I REALLY NEED HIS HELP?

I warned you in the beginning that this would be a very challenging part of our journey into understanding God more. Please understand that asking God to find us a parking spot at a mall and asking God to perform a miracle of healing are two completely different things. It's not that one is easier or more important for God to do. Finding us a parking space does not require God to grant us a rare pardon from the consequences of original sin. But healing us of malignant cancer does.

Doug Robinson, a close family friend and a respected evangelist in my home area of Bancroft, Ontario, was instrumental in leading numerous people to Christ over the years. His tireless dedication to spreading the gospel had resulted in hundreds of changed lives in the generations of several families.

One day the doctors informed Doug that he had malignant cancer of the ureter. (The ureter is a "tube" connecting the kidney to the bladder.) I thought, *If anyone should get a pardon from his cancer, surely it is Doug.* Hundreds and hundreds of prayers went up in our tight-knit community for a miracle. But that miracle of healing never came. Doug, in his early seventies, eventually went under the knife to have the cancer removed. The surgery was deemed successful; however, a series of exhaustive chemotherapy treatments would be needed.

I remember driving Doug to the large cancer center two hours away for a chemotherapy treatment. Ironically, it was the cancer center where I had worked on a skin cancer research project as a medical student. During our ride together, Doug couldn't say enough about his gracious heavenly Father. He stated, "Brad, I have never felt the peace of God in my heart like I did when I was lying on that operating room stretcher about to undergo the cancer surgery. I have no doubt whatsoever that it was due to the power of prayer."

I have seen many a patient waiting on a stretcher ready to undergo major surgery. Some try to joke with the operating room staff to disguise their nervousness. Others allow their anxiety and fear to show by being grumpy and very demanding. Very few, though, appear to have that extraordinary "peace of God" in their hearts that Doug described.

SEEING THE COMPLETE SUNSET

An hour into our road trip, Doug removed his hat, closed his eyes, and prayed, "Dear Father, please help us to find a parking spot when we reach the cancer center." For some people, asking the Almighty for a nearby parking spot would seem rather strange and trivial given the state of chaos our world seems to be in. But Doug still felt a little tired from a previous chemo treatment, and a long walk would not help. When we arrived, sure enough, a parking spot was waiting for us at the doors. This was quite remarkable, considering that only five or six parking positions were close to the main entrance—and the cancer center was filled with dozens and dozens of patients and family members, most of whom would have had a longer trek from a more distant parking lot. In seven trips to the center, Doug prayed every time; and on six occasions he found a spot immediately. The one time he didn't find one right away, he had to wait only five minutes before moving his vehicle in.

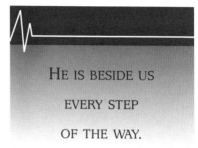

HE IS BESIDE US

EVERY STEP

OF THE WAY.

One doctor told Doug to expect several side effects from the chemotherapy. But Doug did amazingly well. Other than some tiredness, he had few side effects. Very little nausea. And little hair loss. Overall, he felt quite good. Although Doug was able to keep preaching the gospel for more than a year after his treatment, eventually the remission ended, the cancer returned, and Doug went home to meet his Lord and Savior face-to-face. I joined the large congregation at the funeral, where we joined together to sing God's praises and give thanks for the wonderful impact Doug had had on so many of our lives.

Now, God could have completely pardoned Doug from his cancer, but he didn't. Because of God's mercy, medical discoveries have allowed us to prolong lives, diminish pain, and even cure some cancers. Had Doug been born a hundred years earlier, he would surely have died at the onset. Instead of a miracle, though, God likely lessened the consequences of Doug's suffering in response to prayer. When we pray for healing, God may not grant us an instant miracle on the spot. But that doesn't mean our heavenly Father isn't right beside us in our earthly work camps. He is there, all right, *and he is not still!* He is beside us, holding our hands, hugging us close to his chest, crying with us, and grieving with us, every step of the way.

As in Doug's case, our loving heavenly Father may not grant you a miracle. But he may grant the doctors and nurses wisdom in treating your disease. He may give you an indescribable sense of peace like you've never experienced before. He may lessen the side effects of medications and bring you through the surgery with fewer complications. He may even do something as small as finding you a parking spot at a busy hospital. Prayer is undeniably powerful!

Howbeit, some people believe God doesn't really care about finding us parking spots at malls. The King of the universe, they surmise, doesn't bother himself with such petty stuff. If we snag a prized parking spot in front of Wal-Mart, it's most likely a coincidence—or we're unknowingly parked in the handicapped parking spot.

The next story goes far beyond three wishes for a parking spot to touch our hearts.

Recently I received an e-mail from a young man, Joey, asking for urgent prayer.[6] His wife, Katie, who is only twenty-eight, is suffering terribly from metastatic cancer. Her tumors are so large they can be seen protruding from her abdomen. She is having fluid drained from her abdomen and lungs in the hospital where I am currently working. In the e-mail, her heartbroken husband shared yet another setback for his young wife. Katie had developed a blood clot in her left lung and she was struggling for each breath. Subsequently, she could only sleep for a short time in a half-sitting, half-lying position, propped up with pillows or held in this awkward position by her husband, who was getting even less sleep.

After taking sleeping pills one night, Katie developed a bad rash that only added to the discomfort and prevented her from sleeping. Joey cried out to God, asking his heavenly Father to take away the rash. *Why couldn't God answer this one thing,* Joey thought, *so that Katie could sleep this one time?* It seemed like such a small request. But it was at that point Joey felt that his prayers and tears hit an "impenetrable wall."

He shared this from the heart:

> I am accustomed to having God answer me when I pray—
> for wisdom, guidance, insight, and in many other tangible
> situations where I have seen the hand of God work in
> answer to my prayers. Yet last night as I prayed for this one
> small thing, I felt as if there was what felt like an impene-
> trable wall, or an empty void, between my prayers and
> God. I felt as if I were incapable ... to have my prayers
> physically manifested in relief for Katie's condition. This
> greatly disturbed me, for I can find no reason in Scripture
> for this to be so—for prayers for physical comfort and
> relief to be any different than any other sort of prayers.

His e-mail traveled through cyberspace to dozens of Christian friends and family. All around the world we are praying that God will heal Katie of her terminal cancer in a miraculous way. Joey's devotion and faith are so apparent in every e-mail that I wonder why God has not brought physical healing to his beloved wife. As Joey pondered, why does God seem to answer our prayers so often for wisdom, guidance, and insight, yet when someone we love more than anything else in the world is dying, why do we feel as though a giant wall has been dropped in our path, blocking our prayers? Why does there seem to be such a discrepancy between the prayers God *often* answers and those he *sometimes* answers? Why does God, on occasion, not grant the requests that mean the most to us?

You might consider a parking spot to be child's play for God, but when it comes to granting us daily wisdom, understanding, and strength to pull off his sovereign plan, this is serious business. Joey understands how important these prayers are to God. But why wouldn't God answer prayers that are just as important for his wife's healing?

In *Does God Still Do Miracles?* I wrote about God's daily providence— his mind-boggling attention to "millions of details and circumstances" to bring about his perfect sovereign plan for our lives. All this displays God's genius, power, dominion, wisdom, and love much more than "comparatively uncomplicated miracles."[7] God's daily working— finding us parking spots, bringing influential people into our lives at opportune moments, and supplying us with key resources to accomplish his precise goals—requires far more of God's power and genius than any miracle of healing.

As far as I knew, Joey never *demanded* God to heal his wife instantly. However, those who expect God to *always* and *instantly* work miracles on demand are like little children barging into God's courtroom and ordering the Almighty to completely free us from all the curses he pronounced in the garden of Eden. It's demanding God to completely pardon us from the physical consequences of our sins when we don't deserve it. It's telling the supreme ruler of the universe that his justice, his sovereign will, and his glory don't matter. We wouldn't barge into the United States Supreme Court and order the justices to completely pardon someone proved guilty of second-degree murder. Why, then, might we do that in God's court by *demanding* him to instantly pardon us from the physical consequences of our sins?

Turn to almost any religious TV channel these days and you will likely hear these words: "God *wants* to heal you. God *wants* to prosper you. God *wants* to make you rich! God *wants* to end your suffering." If God *wants* to do all these things, then why isn't he doing it? Why are so many godly saints sick? Doesn't God say in Isaiah 46:10, "*My* purpose will stand, and *I* will do all that *I* please"? If God wants to do something but can't, because presumably mankind or Satan has messed things up for him, then God becomes the incompetent and bumbling liar. Those who think God is handcuffed in such a manner hold a very, very low view of God's power and sovereignty. To such people, God is about as sovereign as Tony the Tiger on the Frosted Flakes box.

Who is really "putting God in a box"—or "on a box"?

Whether we like it or not, God remains the chief judge of the universe who allows these curses he pronounced in the garden of Eden to play out every day. But thank God, he is also our friend, comforter, and loving heavenly Father, who intimately knows every aspect of our lives! He knows and feels our pain and our grief. God feels the pain Katie is suffering every night because he dwells inside her. God himself has experienced pain and heartrending loss when he sent his Son to earth to die for our sins. Christ endured every form of suffering possible when he walked the earth. He wept when he discovered that

Lazarus, a close friend, was dead. His heart broke when Peter, whom he loved deeply, denied him. He experienced extreme hunger and thirst in the desert. He endured lashes as deep and excruciating as those that had killed other victims. He suffered the cruelest mode of death achievable when the soldiers drove large spikes into his wrists and ankles and hoisted him up on the cross. John Dawson says that Christ "feels our hurts more deeply than we do because His sensitivity to suffering is so much greater."[8] God understands better than anyone else the pain you may be going through at this moment. He knows exactly the sickness and the numbness you may be experiencing in your deepest grieving. Why? Because he's been there himself. And no one knows us like our heavenly Father.

In Isaiah, we read, "For the LORD comforts his people and will have compassion on his afflicted ones" (49:13b). "Praise be to the God and Father of our Lord Jesus Christ, the Father of compassion and the God of all comfort," writes Paul (2 Cor. 1:3). Our loving Shepherd grants us "endurance and encouragement" (Rom. 15:5) and "comforts us in all our troubles" (2 Cor. 1:4).

> When you pass through the waters, I will be with you; and when you pass through the rivers, they will not sweep over you. When you walk through the fire, you will not be burned; the flames will not set you ablaze. (Isa. 43:2)

No matter what raging waters or wild fires we may pass through on our journey into understanding God, our Good Shepherd is with us every step of the way.

THE FINISHING BRUSHSTROKES

"We have sought refuge and comfort from God's Word," said Ron and Arlene.

The day Vaughn tragically died, Ron and Jayson drove more than two hours in silence north to the small town of Bancroft to tell Arlene and the rest of the family about the death. Ron clearly remembers walking into his parents' home where everyone was staying that night. The first thing he saw when he walked through the door was an old brown plaster plaque hanging on the wall. "I can still see it so plainly," Ron shared with me, thinking back to that dark day. "It said, 'My grace is sufficient for thee' (2 Cor. 12:9). That is a portion of the verse that has really carried me along."

Unlike believers, unbelievers have no access to God's comforting grace—his personal, one-on-one, compassionate hugs. Unbelievers toil away in their earthly "work camps," but God is nowhere around to comfort them. As adopted children of God, we don't deserve to have the consequences of our sin lessened. We don't deserve to have God answer our prayers with a big hug by granting us strength, understanding, and peace. In Ezekiel 18:4 the Lord says, "For every living soul belongs to me.... The soul who sins is the one who will die." (See also Rom. 6:23.) But God, who is rich in grace and mercy, does bestow divine strength upon his beloved children to allow them to bear even the roughest storms. And he does lessen the consequences of our sins in the physical realm. This is all part of the Almighty's gorgeous sunset!

When sixteen-year-old Becki awoke to find her leg had been amputated, God was most likely cradling the teenager in his arms, comforting her heart with a peace that "transcends all understanding" (Phil. 4:7). When her father was bitterly angry with God, thinking the King of kings had abandoned his daughter, God hugged him even tighter. When Steven Curtis Chapman didn't know whether he would ever be able to sing another note, his Creator was using the darkest moments of his suffering to press Steven closer to him. When Doug was lying alone on the operating room table, about to undergo cancer surgery, his heavenly Father was holding his hand, saying, "I am with you to the end, my faithful son." When Joey feels like his prayers for his dying wife have hit an impenetrable wall, God supernaturally breaks though that wall to reveal his loving presence in a most unexpected way. When Greg wakes up every morning with his celiac disease, the Great Physician bestows more than enough grace to get him through the day. When Arlene was being sexually abused, God was right beside her, wiping away the tears as they streamed down her little face. "Fear not, my child. For I am preparing a place for you where no one will ever hurt you again." When Ron could feel his heart "dripping," and Arlene was numb with grief from the deaths of their three sons, God was wrapping his loving arms of grace tightly around the heartbroken pair.

During the darkest moments of our hurt we can't see God, but we can feel our Father's presence. He holds his dear children close to his chest, whispering, "Be still, and know that I am God" (Ps. 46:10a). "I am here for you, my precious child. And I will never, ever leave you. My grace is sufficient, for it is all you will need to get through this hurt."

When we are suffering the devastating loneliness of a divorce, enduring the heartrending grief and confusion of losing a loved one, or suffering the bitter pain of widespread metastatic cancer, we whisper out from the depths of our hearts, "Father, it really, really hurts." Hugging us even closer in these earthly work camps, God, with tears in his own eyes, replies, "I know my precious child. I know...."

Even though we may experience long periods of silence, we can know beyond a shadow of a doubt that God has his arms wrapped snugly around us. God carried Ron, Arlene, and their family through unimaginable tragedy, suffering, and grief to a sunset of hope and renewed faith. Will he not also be faithful in carrying you through whatever adversity you may be suffering? Ron and Arlene's gripping testimony is proof that God's love and grace are more than sufficient, no matter what adversity we may be facing in life.

It has been said, "The key to joy is not God's *presents,* but his *presence.*" And we know by faith, that with our heavenly Father's ever-abiding presence and help, we will get through these tough times.

Our Father's tears and love are the only assurance we need.

WHY DOES GOD ALLOW SUFFERING?

SOLOMON'S CLUE #8

For then you will see, the treasure lies there,
In the mosaic, beautiful and rare....

8
SOLOMON'S CLUES

The fact that Jesus came and suffered and died does not remove pain from our lives. Nor does it guarantee that we will always feel comforted. But it does show that God did not sit idly by and watch us suffer alone. He joined us and in his life on earth endured far more pain than most of us ever will. In doing so, he won a victory that will make possible a future world without pain.[1]

—PHILIP YANCEY

Mary Bowley Peters (1813–1856), who lived to only forty-three years of age, wrote in her passionate hymn the words, "Sorrow makes our hope the brighter."[2] Indeed! Sorrow drives home the truth that Christ also suffered for us to "make possible a future world without pain." Ron and Arlene are confident in the bright hope that they will one day enjoy this

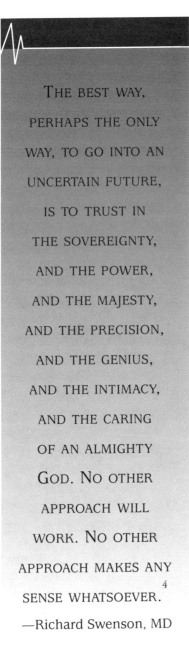

THE BEST WAY, PERHAPS THE ONLY WAY, TO GO INTO AN UNCERTAIN FUTURE, IS TO TRUST IN THE SOVEREIGNTY, AND THE POWER, AND THE MAJESTY, AND THE PRECISION, AND THE GENIUS, AND THE INTIMACY, AND THE CARING OF AN ALMIGHTY GOD. NO OTHER APPROACH WILL WORK. NO OTHER APPROACH MAKES ANY SENSE WHATSOEVER.[4]

—Richard Swenson, MD

glorious world without sickness, death, or tears. They are also confident that one day they will once again see their sons Vaughn, Brent, and Curtis in heaven. Because of their suffering, they understand a little better what Christ went through for them on the cross. They can understand a little more what it was like for the Father to lose his own dear Son. And they can truthfully say, as the writer of Hebrews maintains, "We have this hope as an anchor for the soul, firm and secure" (Heb. 6:19a).

Until we ultimately reach heaven, we must accept by faith that God holds all the answers to our questions. For by faith "we rejoice in the hope of the glory of God" (Rom. 5:2). We place our complete trust in God, knowing that out of our suffering will arise the loveliest mosaic possible, bringing the greatest degree of glory to our heavenly Father. To understand God more, to attain more and more treasures, we must use the lamp of God's Word to illuminate part of this rare and exquisite mosaic—the big picture.

Until we finally reach heaven and see this glorious mosaic in its entirety, we must concur with Steven Curtis Chapman:

> God is God and I am not
> I can only see a part of the picture He's painting
> God is God and I am man
> So I'll never understand it all
> For only God is God[3]

SOLOMON'S CLUE #9

Approaching the end, consider your scene,
    Have you reached leg five, or wedged in between?

BONUS PRIZE

Are you ready for the fifth and final level of intimacy with God?

Everyone likes a bonus—getting something unexpected thrown in. Well, you might consider this last clue of Solomon's to be a bit of a bonus, in a couple of different ways. To begin with, this clue will help us to understand the fifth and ultimate level of intimacy.[†] Sometimes suffering can press us closer to God, but sometimes it can pull us down a rung or two on the intimacy ladder. If your church is like the average church in the United States or Canada, chances are that only a select percentage of the people in your congregation have truly reached this extraordinary level of intimacy in their relationship with God.

Are you one of them?

The second bonus may be even more unexpected: As you grow closer to God, you grow closer to others. The same techniques that

---

†   The first four levels were discussed in *Why Doesn't God Stop Evil?* In *Is God Obsolete?* Solomon presented us with fictional "clues" based on biblical principles just after we won ten million dollars in a highly bizarre game show.

we use to build more intimate relationships with God are the same techniques we use to build more intimate relationships with our soul mates, parents, siblings, and friends. Actually, if you share the journey toward intimacy with God, the closer you draw to your Creator together, the closer you will draw together in your relationship with one another. Guaranteed!

So let's just quickly recap the first four levels of intimacy with God. In *Why Doesn't God Stop Evil?* Solomon's clue was, *"Two small steps forward, three huge leaps recede. Heed the differences, or never succeed."* To succeed past a relationship built merely on clichés and facts, we must heed (or respect and appreciate) the differences that exist between God and us—particularly in regard to our heavenly Father's justice, majesty, and holiness. When one fails to value the individual character traits of the other person in a relationship, often bitterness creeps in because those differences require some sort of compromise in a relationship. To avoid confronting and dealing with these differences, often only mundane facts pass over the breakfast or dinner table:

Reading the junk mail, the husband asks his wife, "What did you do today?"

His wife responds, "I picked up the groceries, watched *The Price Is Right,* and neutered the cat."

"That's nice."

"Yeah."

As in a marriage, "irreconcilable differences" can keep us permanently stuck behind the conflict barrier. "Let God be God" was our motto to help us overcome the trap so many people fall into when they try to eliminate these differences by twisting God into the person *they think he should be.*

We deciphered the important clue, *"On route to triumph, the cup is held out. Drink to discover, beyond any doubt."* Drinking from the cup of salvation involves personally accepting Christ's death on the cross as full payment for our sins. By placing our faith in Christ's atoning work, the Holy Spirit enters, permanently indwelling us "beyond any doubt," allowing for a one-of-a-kind intimacy that can be experienced in no other way.

The next clue read, *"Precedence and awe, intimacy great, The secret is yours, push open the gate."* A major reason why couples never break through the conflict barrier is that they never give "priority status" to their mates. "Honor opens the door to the fourth and fifth levels of intimacy," says Gary Smalley. "And it's a master key."[5] To reach the final levels of intimacy with the Divine we must begin by granting God priority status in every avenue of life. A genuine and healthy fear of God leads to a godly life, and it is the master key that unlocks the door of intimacy in our pursuit for further intimacy with our heavenly Father.

Popping up next was the clue, *"Once through the blockade, the world is anew, But never lodge here, regrets if you do."* This clue from Solomon warns us about the destructiveness of grumbling directly at our Maker (or indirectly by grumbling at others). Every time we gripe and question God's decisions, we take a step backward in our drive for intimacy.

The husband might lash out, "You spent a hundred and fifty dollars to neuter the cat!!"

The wife responds, "He kept running away!"

"I'm going to run away if you keep spending my money like that!"

"*Our* money! When you starting working two jobs like I do, then you can call it *your* money."

Sometimes we grumble at God because of our finances; usually, though, it's because of some trial or suffering we are enduring. This is one way in which suffering can destroy our relationship with God. But it's not God's fault, of course, if we push away from him with our grumbling.

Also in *Why Doesn't God Stop Evil?* was the clue, *"The further you go, the further you taste, To share is the proof—to fear is a waste."* This introduced us to the fourth level of intimacy: *feelings*. Only when our understanding of God has progressed to the stage where we know the true character of our heavenly Shepherd can we feel confident and secure in sharing our feelings with God—whether they be positive or negative.

And now we come to the fifth and final level, which Smalley terms, "The ultimate level of intimacy."

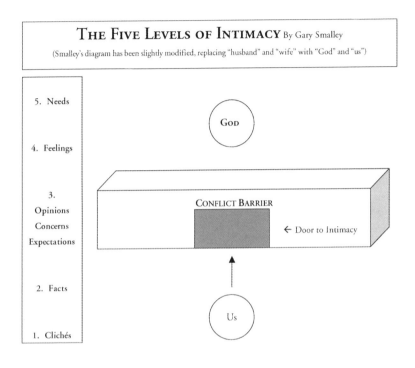

THE FIVE LEVELS OF INTIMACY By Gary Smalley

(Smalley's diagram has been slightly modified, replacing "husband" and "wife" with "God" and "us")

5. Needs

4. Feelings

3. Opinions Concerns Expectations

2. Facts

1. Clichés

GOD

CONFLICT BARRIER

← Door to Intimacy

Us

NEEDS

According to Smalley, a couple has reached the highest level of intimacy when they are able to meet one another's needs (i.e., love, acceptance, honesty, respect, faithfulness, security, sex).

After surveying ten thousand couples, Dr. Smalley found that the number one need for men and women was to have a mate who is honest and trustworthy.[6] In our relationship with God, we, too, have a need for God to be honest, dependable, and trustworthy. But if your stepping-stones are grossly disarranged (a false understanding of the Almighty), it will often appear that God is less than honorable. Your pastor might lead you to believe that God's will is for you to have a trouble-free, stroll-through-the-garden Christian life with no weeds, bugs, gophers, or other pesky afflictions. When your Christian life, however, is less than the fairy-tale existence your pastor promised, usually God's integrity—not your pastor's—takes a beating in your mind. And the intimacy you thought you had with God suddenly vaporizes in a puff of smoke.

> So then, those who suffer according to God's will should commit themselves to their faithful Creator and continue to do good. (1 Peter 4:19)

Never believe, no matter how much you may be suffering, that God isn't faithful. "God is faithful," we read in 2 Corinthians 1:18. "He is the faithful God ..." proclaims Moses (Deut. 7:9). "Your love, O LORD, reaches to the heavens, your faithfulness to the skies," extols David (Ps. 36:5). "O Sovereign LORD, you are God! Your words are trustworthy" (2 Sam. 7:28). When our greatest need was salvation, our altogether faithful and trustworthy God lovingly fulfilled that need by sending his Son to earth to die for our sins. We read in Hebrews 7:26 that Christ "who is holy, blameless, pure, set apart from sinners, exalted above the heavens" is the one who "meets our need." "Let us hold unswervingly to the hope we profess, for he who promised is faithful" (Heb. 10:23; see also 2 Cor. 5:5).

God supplies all our *needs*—not necessarily our *wants*. But as mentioned earlier, God, being the supreme and infinite ruler of the universe, doesn't have any "needs" himself. He does, nevertheless, have *great expectations*. God created us to manifest his glory by asking that we give back to him in a self-sacrificing manner what he originally gave to us: our talents, desires—our entire life—so that we would offer to him in return the praise that is so rightfully due his blessed name.

I challenge you to honestly evaluate where you are in your spiritual life to determine if you have reached the fifth level of intimacy.

Here is a practical checklist:

WHY DOES GOD ALLOW SUFFERING?

The Intimacy Checklist:

- *I am a child of the King.* The first and foremost question you must ask yourself is this: "Have I accepted Christ's death on the cross for payment of my sins and committed my life to him?" If not, then you are not a child of the King, and you consequently have no relationship with the Divine. For we read in John 1:12–13 (NLT), "But to all who believed him and accepted him, he gave the right to become children of God. They are reborn! This is not a physical birth resulting from human passion or plan—this rebirth comes from God."

- *I am being led by the Holy Spirit, bearing fruit for all to see.* "But the fruit of the Spirit is love, joy, peace, patience, kindness, goodness, faithfulness, gentleness and self-control" (Gal. 5:22–23). Read these verses again carefully. If you fall noticeably short in any or all of these nine characteristics, you are probably not filled with the Spirit and do not enjoy the highest level of intimacy with God. If people hold your character in high esteem, perhaps it is because your fruit in the barrel of life is attractive to those looking on (see Prov. 14:29; 17:27). When we model Christ in our lives, usually the only thing the world will hate us for is our love for Christ and his truth.

- *I know without a doubt my eternal destination, and I am not fearful of dying.* The apostle Paul wrote, "For to me, to live is Christ and to die is gain" (Phil. 1:21). If plane crashes and train derailments in the news cause you to live in such fear that you cancel flights or abandon your train trip, then you can't say as the apostle Paul does, "To die is gain." That doesn't mean we take reckless chances with our lives and plunge over Niagara Falls in a barrel. But when the chances of dying are statistically negligible, an intense fear of death mirrors a somewhat dysfunctional relationship with the Divine (see Heb. 2:14–15). If we truly love God, then we will look forward to letting go of this world to be with him (see Titus 2:13).

- *I do not grumble at God, and I hold no grudges, resentment, or hate toward my fellow humans.* "If anyone says, 'I love God,' yet hates his brother, he is a liar. For anyone who does not love his brother, whom he has seen, cannot love God, whom he has not seen" (1 John 4:20). How do you view people from other cultures? How do you view your next-door neighbors—regardless of their skin color? Are you always finding fault with your spouse or your children? Are you continuously saying negative things about people God purposely brings into your life (see Prov. 11:12; 14:21)? If you are, then you likely lack intimacy and understanding of the Divine. Racism, or even an attitude of jealousy toward neighbors and family members, is pure pride, ignorance, and hate. Also, if you don't love and respect your spouse, don't expect God to answer your prayers (see 1 Peter 3:7). Often when we kick God off the throne of our lives, we hop up to take his place, expecting our spouse and family to take a lowly position at our feet. When we sacrificially love God with all of our hearts, we will also love our neighbors and make God's agenda our number one priority.

- *I enjoy following the moral will of God.* "This is love for God: to obey his commands. And his commands are not burdensome" (1 John 5:3). If you deem

God's commands in the Bible to be pure drudgery, you don't love God, and you aren't even close to attaining the fifth level of intimacy (see John 15:10; 21:15–17). Willfully living in sin is the same as telling God you hate him (see Matt. 7:26; 1 John 2:4; 3:10). Do you shun God because you aren't ready to submit to his moral rules? At the other end of the spectrum, if you have fallen into legalism because you lack God's perspective on his priorities in life, then you likely aren't enjoying to the fullest extent the presence of God and the rewards that arise from following God's moral will. Enjoying our service in the court of the King's presence should be our greatest love.

- *I spend more than ten minutes a day in prayer.* You may consider ten minutes to be a low figure (and it is), but you'd be surprised at how many believers don't even take ten minutes a day to talk with their heavenly Father. Prayer should be an ongoing, moment-by-moment, personal conversation with our caring God. If you go several hours, or days, without speaking to your partner, who is sitting in the same room, what does that say about the level of intimacy in your relationship? What would it say about your relationship with God if you did the same? We are instructed to pray to God everywhere (see 1 Tim. 2:8), for everything (see Phil. 4:6), whenever possible (see 1 Thess. 5:17). Communication is the key to any relationship—earthly or divine.

- *Since God's Word is the "joy of my heart" (Ps. 119:111), I am not preoccupied with seeking after supernatural experiences.* Garry Friesen writes: "When one learns to walk by faith rather than by sight, he learns that his fellowship with God is very genuine and personal indeed."[7] Seeking miracles, instead of eagerly striving to cultivate a rich relationship with the Miracle-Worker by way of his Word, demonstrates a childish spiritual existence. When you hear about conferences and services on miracles, angels, or demons, do you make an extra special effort to attend? But when you hear about conferences and services focusing on the character of God, do you stay home? Can you honestly say like the psalmist that God's Word is the "joy of my heart"?

- *I am committed and consistent in my spiritual walk with God.* A "yo-yo" Christian characterizes an on-again-off-again relationship with the Divine. The superficial relationship with the heavenly Father hangs by a string, and every time the Christian lets go of God, he or she quickly drops into the world's playground, spinning around in a useless and disparaging daze of sin. Intimacy with God shouldn't come and go like a yo-yo. It doesn't ride an emotional roller coaster, and it isn't location dependent. Charles Ryrie says, "The easiest place in which to be spiritual is in public; the most difficult is at home."[8] A committed spiritual relationship with God is a stable relationship. And a stable relationship can weather any storm, no matter what direction it hits us from.

- *I have dedicated my life to bringing glory to God—not obtaining material possessions and fame.* You can't intimately hold on to God if you have one hand wrapped tightly around your worldly possessions. Christ says, "No one can serve two masters. Either he will hate the one and love the other, or he will be devoted to the one and despise the other. You cannot serve both God and Money" (Matt. 6:24; see also Phil. 1:21). Materialism and greed are born enemies of God. Do you become a little jealous when you see your friend or neighbor with a new car or home? When you hear about the extravagant money-spending lifestyles of the rich and famous, do you become a little upset or envious, perhaps making a big deal about it? Or do you just ignore it—or laugh about it with a nonchalant attitude? When we put God before our money, what others do with their money is merely amusement for us.

If you can't honestly affirm that the above bullet points are true in your life, then you have likely not reached leg five—the fifth and highest level of intimacy with God that can be achieved here on earth. More than likely, you remain stuck at—or wedged in between—two lower levels, unable to enjoy to the fullest a personal relationship with God. Naturally then, your understanding of the Almighty will be hindered.

As you can see, achieving true closeness with God and spotting divine footprints in your life is not about achieving some elevated, mind-transcending experience that some are striving after today. True intimacy requires true honor, true knowledge, and true time alone with the one true God of the universe. Just as you can't achieve the highest level of intimacy with your spouse overnight on a romantic honeymoon, you can't achieve the ultimate level of intimacy overnight with God in some emotionally supercharged church service. Genuine intimacy grows out of an obedient heart lovingly following day by day the will of God as plainly laid out in the Scriptures.

When you are consistently walking with God, step by step, hour by hour in his moral will, with the highest goal of loving God and bringing maximum glory to his name, you have reached the final and ultimate level of intimacy with your heavenly Father. There is, of course, a sense in which you should commit your life to serve God every day. However, if you feel as though you have to keep continuously rededicating your life to God because your heart keeps growing cold and you keep drifting far from his moral will, then you may need to evaluate whether your relationship with the Divine is more dysfunctional than intimate. God is already faithful; it should be our greatest love to remain consistently faithful to him. The more intimate our relationship is with God, the surer our faith. Intimacy develops understanding, and understanding fosters intimacy; intimacy and understanding are therefore inseparable (see Prov. 9:10). You cannot have one without the other, and you cannot have one *and not have the other.* They feed off each other, growing stronger day by day.

Perhaps, though, you've been trying for years without much success to break through the conflict barrier or move past the fourth level of "feelings" to the fifth and highest level of intimacy. I would be lying to you if I said every believer eventually makes it—or that everyone who reaches the fifth level is able to hang on to that treasured echelon until heaven. I confess that even in recent years as an author there have been times when I've felt discouraged and somewhat distant from God. I spent four years writing this book series during a very long five-year sabbatical from medicine due to bureaucratic incompatibilities in medical licensing between the United States and Canadian governments. There were more than a few times when I became discouraged with God, wondering if he really cared about me, and wondering if I was crazy for spending thousands of hours writing a book series that might never be published when I had just finished eleven years of training to be a medical specialist.

Recently I returned to medicine after my five-year absence. Trying to remember what I had learned more than half a decade earlier, being on call in the hospital, caring for some really sick patients, and performing rewrites on this book series late into the night has been another big challenge in my life. But through all my trials and the strange series of events in my life, God has remained faithful. And I have no reason to believe that he will not continue to be faithful, no matter what he has planned for me.

If you haven't reached the fifth level of intimacy with God, or if you have slipped down a few rungs on the intimacy ladder, thinking that God has forgotten about you, please don't give up! What better time than now to say, "I've had it with my mediocre, lukewarm relationship with God. I'm tired of all the confusion, bitterness, guilt, and monotony in my life. I want to discover and experience a deep-rooted, heart-thumping, life-changing, mind-blowing intimate understanding of my Creator and Lord. I want God's passion to be my passion. I want God's priorities to be my priorities. I want God's love to be my love for others. I've come this far in the journey, and to turn back or stop now would be the biggest mistake of my life. I know the journey will only get tougher from here—but with God's help I'll be prepared for what's coming. For I've counted the cost. I've decided to put God's glory in my life first and everything else a distant second. I've signed a contract with my heart and mind that I'm going to keep arranging and rearranging my "stepping-stones" to more clearly understand God.

And one day I know I will finally hear those precious words from my Lord, "Well done, good and faithful servant!" (Matt. 25:21).

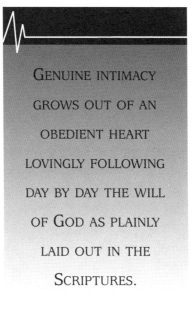

GENUINE INTIMACY
GROWS OUT OF AN
OBEDIENT HEART
LOVINGLY FOLLOWING
DAY BY DAY THE WILL
OF GOD AS PLAINLY
LAID OUT IN THE
SCRIPTURES.

Scenes from the Journey Ahead

Looking back through the pages of this book series, I think you'd have to agree that we've come a long way on our exciting journey into understanding God. We've set our sights squarely on the one true God of the universe. We've grabbed hold of our trusty treasure map for guidance—the authoritative and inerrant Word of God. And with some helpful clues from Solomon, we've spotted the divine paths and persevered past the dangerous obstacles and pitfalls to gain some vital insight into the rich character of almighty God. "Search for it as for hidden treasure," is Solomon's valuable advice (Prov. 2:4).

In the process, we've arranged our stepping-stones into a level path across many raging rivers. Some wild rivers—for example, those centering on the sovereignty of God—we have yet to fully conquer. But using God's Word as our trusted lamp, we've laid down a host of fitting paths, allowing us to at least catch a glimpse of the other side.

WHY DOES GOD ALLOW SUFFERING?

If I were to summarize our journey so far, it would probably be the Lord's own words in 1 Samuel 16:7: "Man looks at the outward appearance, but the LORD looks at the heart." If we could grasp the profoundness of this one verse, it would radically revolutionize every aspect of our lives. No longer would we charge through life thinking that God owes us "Happy Meals." No longer would we consider ourselves to be "morally good people." No longer would we go through life second-guessing God's purpose, priorities, motives, power, majesty, wisdom, justice, judgment, holiness, grace, or goodness. *Gazing at our hearts from God's perspective truly changes everything.*

Our understanding of God has certainly increased ... but the never-ending journey will still continue in the expansive, uncharted land before us. Understanding God, for the dedicated and faithful believer, is truly a day-by-day, hour-by-hour, mind-, heart-, and soul-grappling journey, yielding priceless and unfathomable treasures—sometimes by the minute, sometimes when the saint is least expecting it....

Here's a quick look back at the other books in the series.

IS GOD OBSOLETE?

Nearly everyone at some point in life questions God's ability to run the universe. But are we asking the proper questions, from the proper perspective, based on a proper understanding of the Almighty? What might we have in common with a four-year-old? You might be surprised to discover the similarities as we explore the "personal spirituality" craze overtaking the world. Has God become, in a sense, obsolete? This book in the series is packed with gripping anecdotes and lively illustrations—from trying to resuscitate a gang-banger's exposed heart, to participating in one of the most bizarre futuristic game shows ever concocted. This minibook is a great resource to pass along to believers and nonbelievers alike.

SCENES FROM THE JOURNEY AHEAD

Why Doesn't God Stop Evil?

How often do we look with dismay at the mess in our world and ask, "What was God thinking?" If there really is a good God up above, why is there so much evil in this world? If God is all-powerful, why didn't he bind up or destroy the Devil right from the beginning? If heaven is so great, why didn't God send us straight to paradise and forget earth all together? Where was God on September 11? And where was God when Hurricane Katrina struck? These and many other difficult questions are tackled head-on, providing fresh insight into some of the toughest questions ever asked of the Almighty. When the subject of evil is closely examined, we discover that there is a strong vein of wisdom and compassion in God's justice that Christendom has failed to recognize.

Does God Still Do Miracles?

Much debate lingers over the hot questions: Is God still performing miracles of healing today? If so, how common are they? Many Christian physicians, including me, believe God still performs miracles of physical healing that defy natural explanation. But are the hosts of "miracles" we hear about so often truly miracles? If these faith healings are not true miracles, then how does one explain the thousands of people who are instantaneously getting better? If the diseases being "cured" are not "all in one's head," then what biological mechanisms could possibly explain this phenomenon we're seeing? Why not just give God the benefit of the doubt and label every astonishing healing a miracle? What insights does God provide us in his Word? This book takes seriously Paul's mandate to "examine everything carefully" (1 Thess. 5:21 NASB). Some of the most fascinating and up-to-date medical and investigative research is examined in an attempt to uncover the truth about what is going on in faith-healing services and healing shrines around the world. A new generation of believers wants answers—and *Does God Still Do Miracles?* delivers.

Readers' Guide

For Personal Reflection or Group Discussion

Chapter 1
Suffering: God's Will or the Devil's?

1. Have you or someone close to you ever experienced terrible losses like Andrew? If you have, how did it feel? Did you question God's justice and mercy? Do you think it offends God if we cry out to him in frustration and anger?

2. Was it God's will for Jesus to suffer and die, or was Jesus' suffering and death Satan's victory? What did Jesus tell his disciples about suffering? Why do you think God allows suffering?

3. What does the author say is the cause of the "health and wealth" message of so many preachers today? What can you do if you find

yourself in a church where the pastor is constantly proclaiming this false gospel from the pulpit?

CHAPTER 2
THE "SOVEREIGNTY OF SATAN" LIE

1. Who is in control of the world, God or Satan? What is meant by the term *the sovereignty of Satan*? Where did this teaching come from? Have you ever encountered it or talked to anyone who has?

2. Are most illnesses caused by Satan? What are the true causes of most illnesses?

3. Does God expect us to "bind" Satan? What did God's mightiest creature, the archangel Michael, do in relation to binding Satan? What does the Bible instruct us to do when confronted by Satan?

CHAPTER 3
WHEN OUR CHILDREN DIE

1. What lessons did the author learn from the tragic story of Ron and Arlene and the death of three of their six sons? What lessons have you learned from your own tragedies, or those of close friends?

READERS' GUIDE

2. Have you or someone close to you ever experienced a great loss like Ron and Arlene's? If you are comfortable sharing it, can you tell a little bit about how you or they dealt with it?

3. Have you ever observed Christians condemning other believers because of some tragedy they've experienced? Why do you think Christians sometimes find it difficult to enter into others' sufferings?

CHAPTER 4
"YOU HAVE A LOT OF EXPLAINING TO DO, GOD!"

1. According to the author, who is more likely to have experienced severe suffering: atheists and agnostics, or heroes of the faith? Who do you think has a better understanding of suffering?

2. What are two main reasons we suffer? What was Jewish holocaust-survivor Elie Wiesel's explanation for the evils of the holocaust?

3. C. S. Lewis, Christian author of the beloved children's stories *The Chronicles of Narnia,* said "pain is God's megaphone." What do you think he meant by this? What does Joni Eareckson Tada say about pain and suffering?

4. What reason does Charles Stanley give for many Christians' struggle with adversity? Does this accord with what Ron and Arlene experienced? How or how not?

WHY DOES GOD ALLOW SUFFERING?

CHAPTER 5
IS GOD PUNISHING ME?

1. What are some of the reasons for suffering listed by H. L. Willmington? Which of these strikes you as most relevant to your own experiences of suffering?

2. Does God ever use suffering to chasten us for our sin? What famous Bible story illustrates this? What were some of the consequences that were visited on this Old Testament person, whom God called "a man after my own heart"?

3. According to the author, how frequently does God inflict suffering to chasten people today? How does he explain this apparent "change in strategy" on God's part?

4. What are three other wrong responses about suffering given to grieving people?

5. What was the real reason Job suffered?

CHAPTER 6
THE ULTIMATE REASON WE SUFFER

1. Why is it so difficult for unbelievers to make sense of human suffering? What does suffering have to with God's justice?

2. According to the author, what did the curses from God following the Fall recorded in Genesis reveal about God? What is the source of most of the evils in the world? To God, are such evils as rape and murder any more unjust than the process of aging and death to which we are all subjected?

3. What did God do to remedy the problem of suffering due to sin in the world? If God saw fit to subject his only son to pain, suffering, and death to free us from condemnation, does that provide any consolation for us in our suffering? If so, how? What does it tell us about God?

Chapter 7
Seeing the Complete Sunset

1. In what ways does the illustration at the beginning of the chapter help you understand the relationship between God's justice and mercy? Can you think of any stories from the New Testament that illustrate God's abundant mercy toward his children?

2. How does our suffering greatly restrain evil? What would the world be like if there were no justice (and, therefore, no suffering)? Would it be a better or worse place?

3. What does the author give as an illustration of God's abundant mercy in our world today? Do you agree that the advances he talks about show forth God's mercy? Why or why not? Do you think the story of Doug supports the author's idea about God's mercy, or not?

WHY DOES GOD ALLOW SUFFERING?

What about Joey and Katie's story? Which do we want more, God's presents or his presence?

CHAPTER 8
SOLOMON'S CLUES

1. According to the quote from Philip Yancey that opens this chapter, what does the fact of Jesus' coming into our world and sharing our pain and death do for us? What doesn't it do for us?

2. Do you think it's really true that "sorrow drives home the truth that Christ also suffered for us to 'make possible a future world without pain'"? How does it do that?

3. Which of the author's thoughts about suffering will you find most meaningful the next time you face hardship? What are some ways you can remember that important truth in the midst of your pain?

NOTES

INTRODUCTION
WERE YOU AWAY THEN?

1. David Heller, *Dear God: Children's Letters to God* (New York: Berkley Publishing Group, 1994), 109.
2. Edward Kuhlman, *An Overwhelming Interference* (Old Tappan, NJ: Fleming H. Revell Company, 1986), 18.

CHAPTER 1
SUFFERING: GOD'S WILL OR THE DEVIL'S?

1. As quoted in Kurt de Haan, *Why Would a Good God Allow Suffering?* Discovery Series Booklet (Grand Rapids, MI: Radio Bible Class Ministries, 1990), 3.
2. James Dobson, *Family News from Dr. James Dobson* (August 2001).

3. Hank Hanegraaff, *Christianity in Crisis* (Eugene, OR: Harvest House Publishers, 1993), 263.
4. Some shepherds, in a conscious or unconscious attempt to retain power, will strike fear into the hearts of their sheep by teaching that Satan will attack them with sickness and poverty. To combat the forces of evil, the sheep must stay close to their leader, whom God has supposedly blessed with certain supernatural gifts.
5. Hanegraaff, *Sickness, Suffering, and the Sovereignty of God*, tape C173, 2000.
6. Kenneth Copeland, *Praise-a-Thon*, TBN, April 1988, as quoted in Hanegraaff, *Christianity in Crisis*, 125.
7. Copeland, *Holy Bible: Kenneth Copeland Reference Edition* (Fort Worth, TX: Kenneth Copeland Ministries, 1991), 129 (emphasis in

original), as quoted in Hanegraaff, *Christianity in Crisis,* 338.

8. Hanegraaff, *Christianity in Crisis,* 153.

9. Kuhlman, *An Overwhelming Interference,* 135 (emphasis in the original).

10. John MacArthur, *The Power of Suffering: Strengthening Your Faith in the Refiner's Fire* (Wheaton, IL: Victor Books, 1995), Logos e-book.

11. Bill Lodge, "'Don't follow the world,' Bakker urges: Former televangelist gives commencement address," *The Dallas Morning News,* May 10, 1998, Religion section.

12. Ibid.

13. Nina Shea, *In the Lion's Den* (Nashville: Broadman & Holman Publishers, 1997).

14. For more information on the plight of Christians around the world, see Kate Tsubata, "Where Faith and State Collide," *The World & I* 14 (December 1, 1996): 60, and Ralph Kinney Bennett, "The Global War on Christians," *Reader's Digest,* August 1997, 51–55.

15. As quoted in Ralph Kinney Bennett, "The Global War on Christians," *Reader's Digest,* August 1997, 51-55.

16. As quoted at http://www.apologeticsindex.org/p00.html (accessed January 9, 2005).

17. As quoted in Hanna Rosin, "Personal Spirituality," *The Tampa Tribune,* January 29, 2000, 4.

CHAPTER 2
THE "SOVEREIGNTY OF SATAN" LIE

1. John MacArthur exposes in more detail this erroneous "sovereignty of Satan" mind-set and other unbiblical doctrines coming out of charismatic churches. See John MacArthur, *Charismatic Chaos* (Grand Rapids, MI: Zondervan, 1992), and an answer given to a question transcribed from tape GC 70-22, titled "Questions and Answers–Part 50," transcribed at www.biblebb.com.

2. Benny Hinn, (sermon, World Charismatic Conference, Melodyland Conference Center, Anaheim, CA, August 7, 1992), as quoted in Hanegraaff, *Christianity in Crisis,* 212.

3. E. W. Kenyon, *The Blood Covenant* (Lynnwood, WA: Kenyon's Gospel Publishing Society, 1969), 14, 16, as cited in Hanegraaff, *Christianity in Crisis,* 24, 212. (See also p. 32.)

4. Kenneth E. Hagin, *Word of Faith,* December 1980, 14, as quoted in Rod Rosenbladt, "Who Do TV Preachers Say That I Am?" in Michael Horton ed., *The Agony of Deceit* (Chicago: Moody Press, 1990), 112.

5. Hagin, *Having Faith in Your Faith* (Tulsa, OK: Faith Library, 1980), as quoted in Michael Horton, "The TV Gospel," in Horton, *The Agony of Deceit,* 126.

6. Copeland, "What Happened from the Cross to the Throne" (Fort Worth, TX: Kenneth Copeland Ministries, 1990), tape 02-0017 as quoted in Hanegraaff, *Christianity in Crisis,* 134–35.

7. Wesley L. Duewel, *Touch the World Through Prayer* (Grand Rapids, MI: Francis Asbury Press, 1986), 105.

8. Ibid., 129.

9. Dutch Sheets, *Intercessory Prayer* (Ventura, CA: Regal, 1996), 28.

10. Ibid., 209.

11. Ibid., 141.

12. Peter Kopp and J. Larry Jameson,

"Transmission of Human Genetic Disease," in *Principles of Molecular Medicine*, J. Larry Jameson, ed. (Totowa, NJ: Humana Press Inc., 1998), 43.

13. Philip J. Asherson and Sarah Curran, "Approaches to gene mapping in complex disorders and their application in child psychiatry and psychology," *British Journal of Psychiatry* 179 (2001): 122–28.

14. John MacArthur says, "The apostles were given the authority to bind and loose—speak and act under God's authority—as the foundational representatives for the church. They did not act arbitrarily, nor did they operate apart from the Holy Spirit (see Acts 2:42–47; 4:28–33)." MacArthur's answer was in response to the question, "A church in our neighborhood teaches that Christians should bind Satan. Please explain what the terms 'binding' and 'loosing' refer to in the gospels," available on the Web site http://www.gty.org/bible_faqs/bible _content.php?qa=bindsat.htm (accessed January 16, 2005).

15. From their respective books, *Vine's Complete Expository Dictionary of the Old and New Testament Words; The Bible Exposition Commentary; Matthew Henry's Commentary on the Whole Bible; The MacArthur Study Bible; A Commentary, Critical and Explanatory, on the Old and New Testaments* (Jamieson, Fausset, Brown); *The Handbook to Bible Study; Essential Truths of the Christian Faith; Concise Theology; Institutes of the Christian Religion; The Bible Knowledge Commentary.*

16. Other verses used to argue for this "binding": Jude v. 23; Prov. 24:11; Luke 4:18; Mark 3:27; 16:17; Rom.

16:20. These verses, however, have nothing to do with us binding Satan.

17. John MacArthur, "How to Pray" (Grace Community Church, Panorama City, CA) tape GC 1358, available at www.biblebb.com.

CHAPTER 3
WHEN OUR CHILDREN DIE

1. As quoted in Misty Bernall, *She Said Yes: The Unlikely Martyrdom of Cassie Bernall* (Toronto: HarperCollins, 1999), 2.

2. Interview with Ron and Arlene, November 17 and 24, 2002.

CHAPTER 4
"YOU HAVE A LOT OF EXPLAINING TO DO, GOD!"

1. Warren W. Wiersbe, *Classic Sermons on Suffering* (Grand Rapids, MI: Kregel Publications, 1984), 92, as quoted in Lee Strobel, *The Case for Faith* (Grand Rapids, MI: Zondervan, 2000), 49.

2. Brewster Chamberlin and Marcia Feldman, "The Liberation of the Nazi Concentration Camps 1945: Chapter VII The Chaplains," *U.S. History,* September 1, 1990.

3. See the section, "Provoking the Whirlwind" in the second chapter of *Why Doesn't God Stop Evil?.* C. S. Lewis estimates that 80 percent of our suffering is caused from the blunders of humanity: C. S. Lewis, *The Problem of Pain* (New York: Touchstone Books, 1996), 79. Dr. Charles Stanley estimates that 60–70 percent of the problems he sees as a counselor are because of the sin of the individual or the sin of someone

else: Charles Stanley, *Victory Over Life's Challenges: Winning the War Within; How to Handle Adversity; The Gift of Forgiveness* (New York: Inspirational Press, 1995), 202.

4. John MacArthur, *Why One Way?: Defending an Exclusive Claim in an Inclusive World* (Nashville: W Publishing Group, 2002), 54.

5. As quoted in Paul Lee Tan, "958: Epigram on Cross-Bearing," *Encyclopedia of 7,700 Illustrations* (Garland, TX: Bible Communications, Inc., 1996), Logos e-book.

6. Lindy Warren, "Steven Curtis Chapman's Silent Nights," *Christian Reader*, March/April 2002, 55–59.

7. Steven Curtis Chapman, "Declaration," *Declaration* (Sparrow Records, 2001).

8. Warren, "Steven Curtis Chapman's Silent Nights."

9. Ibid.

10. Lewis, *The Problem of Pain* (New York: Touchstone Book, 1996), 82.

11. Ibid., 82–83.

12. Joni Eareckson Tada, *Larry King Live,* CNN, August 3, 2004. http://www.cnn.com/TRAN-SCRIPTS/0408/03/lkl.00.html (accessed August 9, 2004).

13. Lewis, *The Problem of Pain,* 85.

14. Philip Yancey, *Disappointment with God* (Grand Rapids, MI: Zondervan, 1998), 240.

15. Tada, *Larry King Live.*

16. Randy Alcorn, *Safely Home* (Wheaton, IL: Tyndale House Publishers, 2001), 318.

17. Charles Stanley, *Victory Over Life's Challenges: Winning the War Within; How To Handle Adversity; The Gift of Forgiveness* (New York: Inspirational Press, 1995), 248.

18. As quoted in Henry W. Frost, *Miraculous Healing* (Great Britain: Christian Focus Publications/OMF Publishing, 1999), 40.

19. Warren, "Steven Curtis Chapman's Silent Nights," *Christian Reader.*

20. Ibid.

21. Tada, *Larry King Live.*

22. Ron, Arlene, and the boys have been told countless times that Vaughn and Brent are not in heaven because of their suicides. Some have labeled suicide a form of the "unpardonable sin." It has only been in the past couple years that Ron and Arlene have had no doubts that they will see their sons. Arlene said, "I fully believe that I will see my children in heaven."

23. Stanley, *Victory Over Life's Challenges,* 219.

24. Ibid., 207.

CHAPTER 5
IS GOD PUNISHING ME?

1. H. L. Willmington, *Willmington's Book of Bible Lists* (Wheaton, IL: Tyndale House Publishers, 1987), Logos e-book.

2. Prithi Yelaja, "Amazing Grace," *The Toronto Star,* March 8, 2002, Religion section.

3. Danylo Hawaleshka, "A Tragedy of Errors," *Reader's Digest* (Canada), (December 2003), 74–81.

4. Kuhlman, *An Overwhelming Interference,* 108.

5. James Dobson, *When God Doesn't Make Sense* (Wheaton, IL: Tyndale House Publishers, 1993), 87–88.

6. Some might argue that I'm contradicting what I wrote earlier. Satan wanted to completely destroy Job to get him to curse God. Today, in the declining spirituality of our Western world, Satan has found a much better method to do essentially the same

thing. By trying to make us more prosperous, Satan's goal is to use the god of materialism to turn our hearts away from the one true God. In our day and age, this strategy usually works best.

7. John MacArthur Jr., *The MacArthur Study Bible*, (Nashville: W Publishing Group, 1997), Logos e-book.

8. If God can create a heaven where there is no sin, why couldn't he have created an earth without sin and then created the illusion so that we would have total "free will" from our perspective? Wouldn't this have been in *our* best interests?

9. God entrusts us with trials, but he doesn't need to. He could have raised us all in good Christian homes, blessed us with much wisdom and understanding, given us godly mentors and shaped our lives exactly the way we would think is ideal. Our all-powerful God isn't handcuffed, saying, "The only way I can get my child's attention is to make him suffer. The only way I can turn this person to me is to make him suffer. The only way I can bring this person to me is to make him see a loved one suffering." Not so. Job was already a righteous and upright man before his tragedies hit.

10. It seems likely from the way Job, his wife, and his friends responded to the suffering that this was the first time they had experienced any degree of suffering in their lives. If they had experienced any significant suffering in the past, it would have been mentioned somewhere in all the dialogue that takes place in the book of Job. But it never is.

11. Some might argue that since we cannot fully understand in the first place how our world is better off with evil, then we already battle an endless cycle of unanswerable questions. For the most part, this is true. We can somewhat understand God's justice, but we can't see the big picture completely from God's perspective. Most believers are content, though, in believing that evil is a product of our free will and that our Creator knew what he was doing when he made the existence of evil possible. In the small picture, however, it is much easier to see the pattern of life events and to speculate what could have happened if God had done things a little differently. If one believes that the only reason we suffer is because God needs to work some good in the circumstances, then the personal questions surrounding the small picture are much more intimidating and demoralizing than the universal questions surrounding the big picture.

12. Kuhlman, *An Overwhelming Interference*, 77–78.

CHAPTER 6
THE ULTIMATE REASON WE SUFFER

1. Philip Yancey, *Where Is God When It Hurts?* (Grand Rapids, MI: Zondervan, 1990), 95, as quoted in Brian C. Stiller, *When Life Hurts: A Three-Fold Path to Healing* (Toronto: HarperCollins, 1999), 102.

2. As quoted in Misty Bernall, *She Said Yes: The Unlikely Martyrdom of Cassie Bernall* (Toronto: HarperCollins, 1999), 2.

3. W. E. Vine, Merrill F. Unger, and William White, *Vine's Complete Expository Dictionary of Old and New*

Testament Words (Nashville: Thomas Nelson, 1996), Logos e-book, 54.

4. Some have suggested that the curse of the weeds forced man to work and not sit around idle. With our depraved minds, sitting around idle would have led to much more evil on the earth. Still, the purpose of a curse is not to benefit the person it falls upon.

5. Some believe that the verse, "Christ has redeemed us from the curse of the law," (Gal. 3:13) means that Christ redeemed us from all the curses back in the garden of Eden. But the law, given to Moses, obviously wasn't around in Adam's day. The "curse of the law" spoken of here is the slavery to sin and the curse of eternal death pronounced on all those who would break just one of God's commandments in his law (see Gal. 4:1–7; Heb. 9:14). It is a different curse from the ones leveled upon all mankind back in the garden of Eden.

6. Most authors of books on spirituality try to make people feel better about themselves by downplaying their sinful condition and God's justice. In contrast, the Bible (God's Word) highlights the justice of God and continually emphasizes our state of sinfulness. If God had no part in writing the Bible, do you think humans would have written a book harshly condemning humanity's inbred sin of pride, greed, and lust, with the end result being hell?

7. This "law of chance" is not some bad luck we come by that is outside God's control. Rather, it is random events (from our perspective) of adversity that befall us as part of the curses God pronounced in the garden of Eden. One benefit of this "law of chance" is to keep us humble. (See Eccl. 7:14.)

8. God took Enoch and Elijah to heaven before they had a chance to die. Likewise, when Christ returns for his church, believers will be raptured. These are the only exceptions to the rule, "We will one day all die." Also, not everyone will receive the "same wage" or meet the same destiny in eternity. By God's grace, he has pardoned some from spiritual death to spend eternity with him.

9. John MacArthur, "Biblical Perspective on Death, Terrorism & the Middle East," tape GC 80-240 (Grace to You Ministries, 2001).

10. Ibid.

11. John MacArthur, "How God Uses Suffering, Pt. 2," tape GC 47-84, (Grace to You Ministries).

12. William J. McRae, *A Book to Die For* (Toronto: Clements Publishing, 2002), xviii.

13. Henry W. Frost, *Miraculous Healing* (Great Britain: Christian Focus Publications/OMF Publishing, 1999), 125.

CHAPTER 7
SEEING THE COMPLETE SUNSET

1. Stanley, *Victory Over Life's Challenges*, 236. Emphasis in the original.

2. To the best of my knowledge, this illustration is original. Nevertheless, some parts of it may resemble bits and pieces of other illustrations that various authors have used in the past. (For example, other authors have referred to a fictional country as "Cosmosia" or "Kosmosia.")

3 Stanley, *Victory Over Life's Challenges*, 236.

4. How do we know that such divine

pardons are rare? I don't have exact figures to quote to you, but if you take an honest look around I think you'd have to confess that there is little or no significant difference in the amount of adversity that believers face compared to unbelievers living a similar moral lifestyle. For the most part, believers, like unbelievers, generally suffer the same amount of cancer, heart disease, car accidents, birth defects, burglaries, vandalism, murder, assaults, etc.

5. James Dobson, *When God Doesn't Make Sense* (Wheaton, IL: Tyndale House Publishers, 1993), 86.

6. The names have been changed.

7. MacArthur, *The Power of Suffering*.

8. John Dawson, "The Father Heart of God," http://www.lastdaysministries.org/articles/fatherheart.html (accessed January 16, 2005).

Uncovering the Keys to Life-Long Intimacy (New York: Simon & Schuster, 2000), 124.

6. Ibid., 211–12.

7. Garry Friesen with J. Robin Maxson, *Decision Making & the Will of God* (Sisters, OR: Multnomah Press, 1980), 252.

8. Charles Caldwell Ryrie, *Balancing the Christian Life* (Chicago: Moody Press, 1969), 20–21.

CHAPTER 8
SOLOMON'S CLUES

1. Philip Yancey, *When Life Hurts: Understanding God's Place in Your Pain* (Sisters, OR: Multnomah, 1999), 46. In the strict context, Yancey is speaking of the physical pain Christ endured. We cannot possibly suffer the agony of soul he suffered.

2. Mary Bowley Peters, "Blessed Lord Our Souls Are Longing," *Hymns of Worship and Remembrance*, 228.

3. Steven Curtis Chapman, "God Is God," *Declaration*, (Sparrow Records, 2001).

4. Richard Swenson, MD, *God's Sovereignty*, tape CT261/24369 (Colorado Springs: Focus on the Family, 2000).

5. Gary Smalley, *Secrets to Lasting Love:*

.

Additional copies of *WHY DOES GOD ALLOW SUFFERING?*
and other Victor titles
are available wherever good books are sold.

If you have enjoyed this book,
or if it has had an impact on your life,
we would like to hear from you.

Please contact us at:

VICTOR BOOKS
Cook Communications Ministries, Dept. 201
4050 Lee Vance View
Colorado Springs, CO 80918

Or visit our Web site:
www.cookministries.com

Victor®
The Bible Teacher's Teacher